大学生のための英文法再入門

町田 健＋豊島克己 編著

KENKYUSHA

はじめに

　本書は、高校までに身につけるべき英文法を、大学初期で集中して学べるように編集した英文法学習用のテキストです。大学で使われることに配慮して、例文や問題はできるだけ実用レベルのものを採用しました。本書でしっかり学習してもらえれば、基本的な英文法力が身につくとともに、TOEIC、TOEFLなどの資格試験、大学の原書講読やライティングの授業にもよりスムーズに対応できるようになります。

　大学の英語の授業では、中学・高校で6年間やってきた英語力を前提として授業が進められますが、高校レベルの英文法でつまずいていると、効率的に授業をこなすことができません。英文法がおろそかなままだと、せっかく時間を割いて英語を取り組んでも効果的な学習の妨げになります。大学で英語をしっかり学ぶためにも、基本的な英文法はなるべく早く身につけてください。

　英文法に自信がない人はぜひ本書で英文法を土台からしっかり積み上げ、自信がある人も本書で基本を再確認すると必ず役に立ちます。

※

　本書は全体が15のユニットに分かれています。それぞれ1ユニットに基本的に1つの分野、あるいは関連する分野をまとめて盛りこんでいます。1ユニットあたりの負担は、なるべく均等になるように配慮しています。

　1ユニットは解説と問題に分かれています。問題は、解説に織りこまれているので、解説と問題は複数のパートに分かれ、基本的には解説→問題を何度か繰り返す形で取り組む構成です。

　解説では、まず英文法用語など最低限の情報を頭に入れ、次に例文を通して頭に入れた情報を確認しながら、例文の構造や意味を理解してください。例文で不明な点があれば必ず解説に戻るといいでしょう。

　なお、例文の単語がわからない場合は、和訳をもとにして、その単語の意味に当てていってもかまいませんが、できればそのつど辞書を引いて、発音とともに覚える手間をかけると、効果が高まります。とくに発音は最初に正確に身につけておかないと、あとで矯正しなければならなくなり、かえって時間がかかります。実用的な英語力をつけるために、ぜひ単語もしっかり押さえてください。

　問題では、穴埋め選択問題を中心に採用しています。選択問題は正誤がはっきりしていて学びやすい反面、答えを適当に選ぶこともできるので、自分の弱点が見えにくい面もあ

ります。力をつけるためにも、問題を解くと同時に、その英文全体の意味がわかるかどうかもチェックしてください。わからないところは必ず確認して、可能なら繰り返し声に出して読んで、英文ごと丸暗記することをおすすめします。

「英文法学習は理屈が半分で慣れが半分」と言われることがあります。本書もまさに解説が半分、問題が半分の構成です。理解したあとは、例文や問題を繰り返しやって慣れることで身につけましょう。

※

本書を編むに際しては、英語教師の立場から豊島がグランドデザインと問題作成を担当して、それを受けて、イギリス人作家のクリストファー・ベルトン先生が英文校閲を、言語学者の町田が解説や構成の加筆修正などをおこないました。それぞれ違った立場から意見を交換して、実用的でかつ質の高いテキストに仕上げたつもりです。

本書を皮切りに、英語をもっと効率的に、いや、願わくば、もっと楽しんで英語に取り組んでいただけたら、著者としてこれにまさる喜びはありません。

2014年秋　著　者

目　　次

はじめに iii

Unit 1　　動詞の基礎と文型 1

Unit 2　　動　詞 2 9

Unit 3　　時　制 15

Unit 4　　助動詞 24

Unit 5　　名詞、冠詞、代名詞 33

Unit 6　　形容詞と副詞 40

Unit 7　　態 49

Unit 8　　否定・疑問 59

Unit 9　　準動詞 1 72

Unit 10　 準動詞 2・接続詞 81

Unit 11　 関係詞 88

Unit 12　 形容詞的修飾語句と副詞的修飾語句 99

Unit 13　 比　較 104

Unit 14　 仮定法 113

Unit 15　 倒置、要素の移動、強調、省略 120

Unit 1
動詞の基礎と文型

1-1 主語と動詞

1つの文には、原則として主語と動詞が1つずつ含まれています。また、文の中の主語に対応する動詞を「述語動詞」と呼び分けることがあります。動詞は大きく、一般動詞とbe動詞に分類されます。1つの文の中では、一般動詞もしくはbe動詞のどちらかが、述語動詞として1つだけ用いられるということに注意しましょう。

> 1　I apologize for my rudeness.
> 　　S　V
> 　　私はあなたに自分の不作法を謝ります。
> 2　The movie we saw yesterday was boring.
> 　　　　　　S　　　　　　　　　V
> 　　私たちが昨日見た映画は退屈だった。
> 3　The sun rises in the east and sets in the west.
> 　　　S　　V₁　　　　　　　　　V₂
> 　　太陽は東から出て西に沈む。

1のように主語が1つの単語からなる場合と、2のThe movieや3のThe sunのように複数の単語からなる場合があります。複数の単語が主語であることを示すために、「主語」ではなく「主部」という用語を用いることがあります。

1では、主語がIで、動詞がapologizeです。2では、The movie we saw yesterdayが主部で、wasが動詞です（途中にあるwe saw yesterdayはwhich we saw yesterdayのwhichが省略されているもので、The movieを修飾する関係代名詞節です）。3では、The sunが主部で、risesとsetsが動詞です。このように、andやorなどの接続詞（等位接続詞）を用いれば、1つの文に複数の動詞を並列させることができます。

Exercise 1　以下の英文を全訳し、主語と動詞（述語動詞）を指摘しましょう。

(1) The flight to New York left on time.
(2) A cute girl with blond hair suddenly stood up.
(3) The products made by the company lack reliability.
(4) For decades, the Boeing 747 was the queen of the skies.
(5) Though the lecture was boring, the students tried to look interested.
(6) Those who have had the misfortune to be born poor sometimes make a lot of effort to become rich.

(7) The maintenance work needed to prepare the road for the rainy season is scheduled to begin in a few weeks.

(8) The development of medicine accelerated by new technology has made it possible to cure most diseases.

1-2　一般動詞の変化（現在時制）

現在時制では、主語が単数か複数かで、動詞の変化形が異なります。

learn〈学ぶ〉	単数	複数
1人称	I learn	we learn
2人称	you learn	you learn
3人称	he / she / it learns	they learn

英語の一般動詞の変化は、他のインドヨーロッパ系の言語の変化と比べると、比較的単純です。3人称単数に s をつけるだけで、その他は原形と同じです。ただし、語尾が -o、-ss、-sh、-ch、-x で終わる語は -es をつけて3人称単数形を作ります。

1　The professor teaches us English.　その教授は私たちに英語を教えている。
2　She misses her family.　彼女は自分の家族がいなくて寂しいと思っている。
3　Tom goes to church every Sunday.　トムは日曜日はいつも教会に行く。

have の3人称単数形は has です。

Exercise 2　以下の英文の与えられた動詞を現在時制の適当な形に変化させ、英文を訳しなさい。なお、そのままの形で用いられるものもあります。

1　The temperature often (go) down below minus 30 degrees Celsius here in winter.

2　Water (boil) at 212 degrees Fahrenheit.

3　You (look) good in those clothes.

4　Your suggestion (sound) nice.

5　Permissive parents (spoil) their children.

6　This refrigerator (smell) of rotten fish.

7　John and Jill often (quarrel) with each other.

8　He will call me when he (finish) the job.

1-3　be動詞の変化（現在時制）

	単数	複数
1人称	I am	we are
2人称	you are	you are
3人称	he is / she is / it is	they are

　be動詞は「〜である」「ある」「いる」などの意味を表します。また述語が形容詞のときはbe動詞とともに用います。

1　I am an astronomer.　私は天文学者だ。
2　Are you interested in sociology?　あなたは社会学に興味がありますか。
3　She is really attractive.　彼女は実に魅力的だ。
4　We are worried about the effects of social media on kids.
　　私たちはソーシャルメディアの子どもたちへの影響を心配している。
5　You are hard-working students.　あなたたちはよく勉強する学生だ。
6　They are reliable employees.　彼らは信頼できる従業員だ。
7　She is not at home now.　彼女は今家にいない。
8　The document is in the drawer.　その書類は引き出しの中にある。

Exercise 3　be動詞を適切な形にして空所に入れて、現在時制の英文を作りなさい。また、全体を和訳しなさい。

1　She (　　) a cabin crew member.

2　(　　) this your vehicle?

3　They (　　) my colleagues.

4　I (　　) indifferent to politics.

5　We (　　) satisfied with the result.

6　The professor (　　) not tolerant of lazy students.

7　These girls (　　) my nieces.

8　I believe that he (　　) innocent.

1-4　文型

　英語の基本的な文型は5つです。文型を構成する要素は、主語 (S)、動詞 (V)、目的語 (O)、補語 (C) です。名詞、形容詞、動詞は文型を構成する要素になりますが、副詞、前

置詞句は文型を構成する要素になりません。また形容詞が名詞を修飾している場合は、その名詞は文型を構成する要素になりますが、形容詞は文型を構成する要素にはなりません。

① 第 1 文型 (SV)

1 Time flies like an arrow.　時間は矢のように過ぎる（光陰矢のごとし）。
   S   V

2 Prices will rise if the tax is hiked.　税金が上がったら物価も上がるだろう。
   S   V

3 Is there a room available for tonight?　今晩泊まれる部屋はありますか。
   V   S

② 第 2 文型 (SVC)

1 Great Britain was once part of the European Continent.
   S   V   C

   大ブリテン島はかつてヨーロッパ大陸の一部だった。

2 She looks young for her age.　彼女は年齢の割には若く見える。
   S   V   C

3 This room smells musty.　この部屋はかび臭い。
   S   V   C

4 The paper feels rough.　この紙はざらざらした手触りだ。
   S   V   C

5 The airline company went bankrupt last year.　その航空会社は去年破産した。
   S   V   C

6 He stays calm whatever happens.　彼は何が起ころうと落ち着いている。
   S V   C

③ 第 3 文型 (SVO)

1 I am going to leave Los Angeles for Las Vegas.
   S V   O

   私はロサンゼルスを発ってラスベガスに行くつもりだ。

2 I owe my success to Mr. Clinton.　私が成功できたのはクリントン氏のおかげだ。
   S V   O

3 I had a substantial breakfast.　私は十分な朝食をとった。
   S V   O

4

④ 第4文型（SVOO）

1　He told his friend a story about his trip to China.
　　S　V　　O　　　　O

　　彼は友人に中国への旅行についての話をした。

2　My friend lent me some money.　私の友人が私にお金を貸してくれた。
　　　S　　　V　O　　O

3　Shall I make you some tea?　お茶でもお出ししましょうか。
　　　　S　V　 O　　O

⑤ 第5文型（SVOC）

1　He found the lecture too difficult.　彼はその講義があまりに難しいと思った。
　　S　V　　　O　　　　C

2　Keeping early hours makes a person healthy.　早寝早起きをすると人は健康になる。
　　　　S　　　　　V　　　O　　　C

3　They consider the plan feasible.　彼らはその計画が実行可能だと考えている。
　　S　　V　　　O　　　C

4　She kept me waiting in the rain for an hour.　彼女は雨の中1時間私を待たせた。
　　S　V　 O　　　　　C

　第1文型は、文の要素が主語と動詞であるものです。be 動詞が第1文型を作ることがありますが、その場合の be 動詞は「ある」「いる」「存在する」などの意味を表します。

　第2文型と第3文型は、動詞の後ろに要素が1つだけあるという共通点があります。be 動詞やそれと同じ働きをする動詞の後ろに要素があれば第2文型です。このとき動詞は、主語と後ろの要素を結びつける働きをしています。つまり、主語がどのようなものなのか、あるいは主語がどのような性質を持つものなのかを補語で表すのが第2文型です。She looks young.（彼女は若く見える）という文は、主語である she（彼女）が、young（若い）という性質を持っているように見えるという意味を表します。

　それに対して、第3文型は、主語が目的語に対して何らかの作用を及ぼすことを表します。このため、主語と動詞の後ろの要素を be 動詞で結びつけても正しい文にはなりません。I had breakfast. の had を be 動詞に置き換えて、I was breakfast. にすると、「私は朝食だ」という不自然な意味の文になります。

　第4文型と第5文型は、動詞の後ろに要素が2つあるという共通点があります。第4文型は、第3文型と同じように、主語が目的語に対して作用を及ぼすことを表しますが、さらに、その作用の結果目的語が移動する到達点も表されます。作用の対象が「**直接目的語**」で、目的地が「**間接目的語**」です。My friend lent me some money. という文は、主語である my friend（私の友人）が、直接目的語である some money（いくらかのお金）に対して、

lend（貸す）という作用を及ぼし、その結果目的語のお金が、間接目的語である me（私）に届いたという意味を表しています。

　第 5 文型は、主語が目的語に作用を及ぼして、**目的語が補語のような状態になる**、あるいは**補語のような性質だとわかる**という意味を表します。目的語が補語の状態になるわけなので、目的語と補語を be 動詞でつなぐことができます。He found the lecture difficult.（彼はその講義が難しいと思った）という文は、主語である he（彼）が目的語である the lecture（その講義）に find（わかる）という作用を及ぼして、目的語が difficult（難しい）という性質を持つことがわかるという意味を表します。言い換えると「彼」には the lecture is difficult（その講義は難しい）ということが「わかった」ということです。

Exercise 4　　以下の英文を訳して、文型を答えなさい。

(1)　His voice sounded strange on the phone.
(2)　A moment's hesitation may cost a pilot his life.
(3)　Please keep us updated on our competitors' activities.
(4)　The government's policy on the health insurance system drew a lot of criticism.
(5)　My hometown lies beyond those steep mountains.
(6)　Fruit flies like bananas.
(7)　After the car hit the boy, he remained unconscious for two days.
(8)　The car pulled up right in front of us.
(9)　Could you please leave us alone?
(10)　I wished him a safe and prompt return.

1-5　自動詞と他動詞

　日本語の「上げる」と「上がる」を考えてみましょう。「上げる」は「顔を上げる」のように、「〜を」という目的語を要求します。目的語を要求する動詞が**他動詞**です。「上がる」の方は「賃金が上がる」のように主語と動詞だけで文が成立し、例えば「顔を上がる」のように「〜を」で表される目的語をとることができません。目的語を必要としない動詞が**自動詞**です。

　次に自動詞と他動詞を使った例を見てみましょう。

1　My back hurts.（自動詞）　私は背中が痛い。
2　I go to school every day.（自動詞）　私は毎日学校に通っている。
3　I eat lunch at the cafeteria.（他動詞）　私はそのカフェテリアで昼食を食べる。
4　We discussed the issue in class.（他動詞）　私たちは授業でその問題を議論した。

　英語の他動詞と自動詞がそのまま、日本語の他動詞と自動詞に対応するわけではありません。英語の自動詞には次のような性質があります。

① 動詞で文を終えることができる。
② 後ろに直接、名詞を置くことができない。

　これに対して、動詞の後ろに直接、名詞を置くことができるものが他動詞です。ただし、多くの動詞には他動詞用法と自動詞用法の両方があります。以下自動詞は圓、他動詞は個と表記することにします。

　たとえば、hide には圓「隠れる」と個「隠す」のように、自動詞と他動詞の用法がありますし、compare には個「比べる」と圓「比べられる」という意味があります。例文1の hurt も圓では「痛む」、個では「傷つける」という意味を表します。

　自動詞と他動詞の形が似ている次の2組の動詞にも注意しましょう。

・lie-lay-lain「圓横たわる、ある」
・lay-laid-laid「個横たえる、置く」

・rise-rose-risen「圓上がる」
・raise-raised-raised「個上げる」

　また他動詞であることに注意しなければならない動詞があります。marry は marry her で「彼女と結婚する」という意味を表し、marry *with* her のように余計な前置詞を入れることはできません。

(a) about が不要

　about が不要な要注意動詞には、discuss（議論する、話し合う）、mention（言及する）、consider（考える）などがあります。

> ○ We discussed the matter.
> × We discussed *about* the matter.
> 　私たちはその問題について話し合った。

(b) to が不要

　to が不要な要注意動詞には answer（答える）、approach（近づく）、defy（反抗する）、disobey（背く）、obey（従う）、oppose（反対する）、reach（到着する）などがあります。

> ○ She answered the question.
> × She answered *to* the question.
> 　彼女はその問題に答えた。

(c) with が不要

　with が不要な要注意動詞には confront（直面する）、face（直面する）、marry（結婚する）などがあります。

> ○ They face a problem.
> × They face *with* a problem.
> 　彼らは問題に直面している。

　文型の点から見ると、第1文型と第2文型で用いられる動詞が自動詞で、第3～5文型で用いられる動詞が他動詞です。また、英語の他動詞には「～させる」という使役的な意味が含まるものが数多くあります。surprise（驚かせる）、excite（興奮させる）、satisfy（満足させる）、disappoint（失望させる）などの他動詞は受動態にすることによって、人が「～する」という意味を表します。

> 5　I was surprised at the news.　私はその知らせを聞いて驚いた。
> 6　She is satisfied with her success.　彼女は自分の成功に満足している。

Exercise 5　空所に入れるのに最も適当なものを選んで文を完成させなさい。

(1)　Living costs (　　) almost 2% since last April.
(a) has been risen　(b) has risen　(c) have risen　(d) raised

(2)　Nothing in the world compares (　　) a mother's love.
(a) to　(b) by　(c) for　(d) against

(3)　Let's discuss (　　).
(a) the problem　(b) of the problem　(c) to the problem　(d) about the problem

(4)　The professor (　　) the hypothesis in the previous lecture.
(a) mentioned　(b) mentioned about　(c) mentioned in　(d) mentioned of

(5)　Brian is going to (　　) one of his colleagues.
(a) be married　(b) get married　(c) marry　(d) marry with

(6)　There are some people who (　　) any idea, whether it is good or not.
(a) oppose　(b) oppose to　(c) opposed against　(d) opposed

(7)　The soldiers refused to (　　) the order.
(a) cling　(b) comply　(c) obey　(d) stick

(8)　How do you (　　) such wonderful tomatoes in your garden?
(a) bring on　(b) bring　(c) grow　(d) grow up

(9)　The English teacher (　　) at her good command of English.
(a) alarmed　(b) surprised　(c) astonished　(d) marveled

Unit 2
動　詞 2

2-1　目的語としての動詞

　動詞が別の動詞の目的語になる場合、to 不定詞、動名詞（-ing 形）のいずれかの形にします。原形のまま動詞の目的語として用いることはできません。

> 1　I want to travel abroad.　私は海外旅行をしたい。
> 2　I finished reading the book.　私はその本を読み終えた。

　動詞を目的語にとる動詞は、次の 4 つに分類されます。

① 動名詞のみをとる動詞
admit「認める」、avoid「避ける」、consider「考える」、deny「否定する」、dislike「嫌う」、enjoy「楽しむ」、escape「免れる」、fancy「想像する」、finish「終える」、give up「やめる」、imagine「想像する」、mind「気にする」、miss「免れる」、postpone「延期する」、practice「練習する」、propose「提案する」、put off「延期する」、quit「やめる」、recommend「勧める」、stop「やめる」、suggest「ほのめかす」

② to 不定詞のみをとる動詞
agree「合意する」、crave「切望する」、dare「敢えて〜する」、decide「決心する」、determine「決心する」、desire「望む」、expect「期待する」、fail「〜し損なう」、happen「たまたま〜する」、hesitate「躊躇する」、learn「学ぶ」、manage「どうにか〜する」、offer「申し出る」、plan「計画を立てる」、pretend「ふりをする」、promise「約束する」、refuse「断る」、seek「求める」、wish「望む」、(would) like「望む」

③ to 不定詞と動名詞の両方をとり、意味がほぼ同じになる動詞
attempt「企てる」、begin「始める」、bother「わざわざ〜する」、continue「続ける」、cease「やめる」、hate「嫌う」、intend「するつもりである」、like「好む」、love「大好きだ」、prefer「好む」、start「始める」

④ to 不定詞と動名詞で意味が異なる動詞
・forget to do「〜することを忘れる」／ forget doing「〜したことを忘れる」
・go on to do「引き続いて〜する」／ go on doing「〜し続ける」
・need to do「〜する必要がある」／ need doing「〜される必要がある」
・remember to do「〜することを覚えている」／ remember doing「〜したことを覚えている」
・regret to do「残念ながら〜しなければならない」／ regret doing「〜したことを後悔する」

・try to do「～しようとする」／try doing「試しに～する」

> 3　I forgot to tell them the news.　そのニュースを彼らに言うのを忘れた。
> 4　I will never forget seeing you here.　ここであなたに会ったことを決して忘れない。
> 5　I regret saying a thing like that.　そのようなことを言ったことを後悔している。
> 6　I regret to say that you are sacked.　残念ながらあなたはクビだとお伝えします。

「～が必要だ」という意味を表すためには、need または want を用います。ただし、need［want］to do は「～することが必要だ」、need［want］doing は「～されることが必要だ」という受け身の意味になります。

> 7　He needs to take a rest.　彼は休憩することが必要だ。
> 8　The car needs fixing.　その車は修理の必要がある。

8の fixing を不定詞に置き換えると to be fixed になります。このように、無生物が主語の場合、「need＋動名詞」は「～される必要がある」という受け身の意味を表します。この意味で want を使うこともできますが、まれにしか用いられません。need の代わりに require を用いて、The car requires fixing. とすることもできます。

形容詞 sure も、不定詞を用いる場合と動名詞を用いる場合で意味が変わってきます。be sure to do は「きっと～する」という意味で、ある事柄が起きることを話し手が確信しているということです。be sure of doing は「～を確信している」という意味で、ある事柄が起きることを主語（＝人）が確信しているということです。

> 9　He is sure to get through the test.
> 　　彼はきっと試験に合格する。※確信しているのは話者。
>
> 10　He is sure of getting through the test.
> 　　彼は試験に合格すると確信している。※確信しているのは「彼」

Exercise 1　空所に入れるのに最も適当なものを選んで文を完成させなさい。

(1)　I am planning (　　) my grandfather's house in Hokkaido.
(a) as I will visit　(b) for visiting　(c) that I visit　(d) to visit

(2)　I'm considering (　　) this company.
(a) quit　(b) quitting　(c) to quit　(d) to have quit

(3)　I can't imagine her (　　) in New York.
(a) to work　(b) to be working　(c) working　(d) work

(4)　After my pet cat died, I (　　) to think more seriously about the meaning of life.

(a) became (b) coming (c) caused (d) started

(5) It is often hard to remember (　) vitamin pills three times a day after meals.
(a) to take (b) taking (c) to have taken (d) to be taken

(6) The lecturer recommended (　) a number of books before the exam.
(a) reading (b) that we would read (c) to read (d) to us to read

(7) Don't (　) to knock. Walk straight in.
(a) treat (b) surprise (c) offend (d) bother

2-2　主語＋動詞＋目的語＋to 不定詞

目的語のあとに to 不定詞をとる代表的な他動詞を確認しましょう。

> 1　I want you to clean your room immediately.
> 　　私はあなたに自分の部屋をすぐに掃除してほしい。
> 2　My mother forced me to practice the piano
> 　　私の母は私にピアノの練習をするよう強制した。

　ほとんどの場合、目的語は to 不定詞の意味上の主語になっています。1 では掃除をするのは「あなた」であり、2 ではピアノの練習をするのは「私」です。ただし、to 不定詞の主語が文全体の主語になる場合もあります。

> 3　You promised me to buy the bag.　あなたは私にそのバッグを買ってくれると約束した。

　「バッグを買う」のは主語の You です。

★「主語＋動詞＋目的語＋to 不定詞」の形をとる代表的な動詞
advise「～するように忠告する」、ask「～するように言う、頼む」、encourage「～することを励ます」、urge「～することを促す」、get「～させる」、invite「～するように誘う」、lead「～するように導く」、expect「～するものと思う」、require「～するように要求する」、allow「～することを許す」、permit「～することを許可する」、force「～することを強いる」、forbid「～することを禁じる」、enable「～することを可能にする」、tell「～するように言う」、teach「～することを教える」

Exercise 2　空所に入れるのに最も適当なものを選んで文を完成させなさい。

(1) The boy begged his parents (　) the toy for him.
(a) bought (b) buy (c) should buy (d) to buy

(2) Father would not (　) us to borrow the car last night.
(a) consent (b) let (c) agree (d) permit

(3) If I had a day's holiday, it would (　) me to visit my grandmother in Osaka.
(a) enable (b) make (c) have (d) assure

(4) Can you (　) to go to the dentist tomorrow? I forgot my appointment last week and don't want to forget to go again.
(a) remember (b) remember me (c) remind (d) remind me

(5) The nurse (　) enter the room because the patient was in a critical condition.
(a) said us not to (b) talked us not to (c) told to us not to (d) told us not to

(6) Be reasonable — you cannot expect her (　) all the work on her own.
(a) do (b) does (c) did (d) to do

(7) My parents (　) me to go out with the boy.
(a) banned (b) forbade (c) inhibited (d) prevented

(8) He (　) me to participate in the meeting after school.
(a) informed (b) suggested (c) made (d) invited

2-3　知覚動詞

　see（見える）、look at（見る）、watch（見る）、hear（聞こえる）、listen to（聞く）、observe（観察する）、notice（気づく）、feel（感じる）などを知覚動詞といいます。知覚動詞はしばしば以下のような構文をとります。

　　　主語＋動詞＋目的語＋現在分詞（doing）
　　　　　　　　　　　　原形不定詞（do）
　　　　　　　　　　　　過去分詞（done）

　目的語の後ろに現在分詞（-ing 形）がくるか、原形がくるかで、意味に大きな違いはありません。目的語とそれに続く動詞の間に「目的語が〜する」という能動の関係が成立している場合には、SVO doing / do となり、目的語とそれに続く動詞の間に「目的語が〜される」という受動の関係が成立している場合には SVO done という形をとります。

> 1　I heard her playing the violin.　彼女がバイオリンを弾いているのが聞こえた。
> 2　I heard her play the violin.　彼女がバイオリンを弾くのが聞こえた。
> 3　I heard my name called.　自分の名前が呼ばれるのが聞こえた。

2-4　使役動詞

　使役動詞は、知覚動詞と同様に目的語とそれに続く動詞の間に「目的語が〜する」という能動の関係が成立していれば、SVO do の形で用いられます。
　使役動詞は make、have、let の 3 つです。動詞 help（助ける）は、「人が〜するのを助け

る」という意味では SVO to do という構文をとりますが、不定詞の前の to は省略されることが多く、これを使役動詞に含めることもあります。

> 1 They made me go there against my will.
>   彼らは私の意志に反して、私をそこに行かせた。
> 2 They had me go there on their behalf.
>   彼らは自分たちの代わりに私をそこに行かせた。
> 3 They let me go there as I wanted to.
>   私がそうしたかったので、彼らは私をそこに行かせた。
> 4 They helped me (to) go there.　彼らは私がそこに行く手助けをしてくれた。
> 5 They got me to go there on their behalf.
>   彼らは自分たちの代わりに私がそこに行くように頼んだ。

　使役動詞が表す意味はそれぞれ違います。make は強制的に行為をさせること、have は（しばしば目下の）相手に頼んで行為をしてもらうこと、let は「したいようにさせる」「なるがままに放置しておく」という意味を表します。
　目的語と動詞の間に「目的語が〜される」という受動の関係が成立している場合、make と have、get は SVO done のように目的語に過去分詞が後続する構文をとりますが、let の場合は、SVO be done のように過去分詞の前に be を置く構文をとります。
　なお、get O to do も使役の意味を表します。

> 6 I couldn't make myself understood in English.
>   私は英語で自分を理解させることができなかった。
> 7 How much will it cost to have the engine fixed?
>   そのエンジンを修理してもらうのにどれくらいかかりますか。
> 8 I let my friend be picked on by the boys.
>   私は自分の友人がその少年たちにいじめられるのを放置しておいた。

Exercise 3　空所に入れるのに最も適当なものを選んで文を完成させてください。

(1) I hear you and my sister sometimes (　　) on the phone at midnight.
(a) talk　(b) talks　(c) to talk　(d) be talking

(2) 　A: Where are Bob and Susan?
　　　B: I saw (　　) television in the family room a few minutes ago.
(a) them to watch　(b) them watching　(c) they watch　(d) they watching

(3) I fearfully watched an airplane on fire (　　).
(a) land　(b) lands　(c) landed　(d) had landed

(4)　She felt her heart (　　) with great joy.
(a) beat (b) beaten (c) to beat (d) to be beating

(5)　Today we hear it (　　) on all sides that the economy is starting to recover.
(a) says (b) said (c) say (d) saying

(6)　This dress makes me (　　) fat.
(a) seen (b) see (c) look (d) looked

(7)　He said he would (　　) his students participate in the drama contest.
(a) ask (b) force (c) have (d) tell

(8)　Mary's father will not (　　) her do any part-time work until after her exams are over.
(a) allow (b) consent (c) let (d) permit

(9)　John had his driver's license (　　) for speeding.
(a) suspend (b) to suspend (c) suspended (d) suspending

(10)　I got my colleagues (　　) me with the presentation.
(a) help (b) to help (c) helping (d) being helping

(11)　I think I have to get my cell phone (　　).
(a) repair (b) repaired (c) repairing (d) to repair

Unit 3
時　制

3-1　現在形、過去形、進行形

動詞は**動作動詞**（action verb または dynamic verb）と**状態動詞**（stative verb または static verb）に区別されます。状態動詞とは、恒常的な性質、思考や感情を表す動詞であり、動作動詞とは運動や変化を表す動詞です。代表的な状態動詞には look（見える）、smell（〜なにおいがする）、taste（〜な味がする）、seem（〜だと思われる）、appear（〜に見える）、have（持つ）、own（所有する）、possess（所有する）、agree（合意する）、like（好む）、know（知る）、depend（依存する）、need（必要とする）、remember（覚えている）、want（欲する）、exist（存在する）、resemble（似ている）、belong（属する）、contain（含む）などがあります。

また、代表的な動作動詞には go（行く）、come（来る）、walk（歩く）、speak（話す）、eat（食べる）、make（作る）、take（持って行く）、run（走る）、study（勉強する）などがあります。

① 現在形

現在形は、現在起きている事柄や、現在の習慣、一般的な真理などを表します。状態動詞は原則として進行形にすることはできず、現在の状態を現在形で表します。

> × I am knowing her.
> ○ I know her.
> 私は彼女を知っている。

動作動詞が現在形で用いられるのは、習慣、不変の真理、客観的記述、スポーツ中継などの場合です。

> 1　The earth goes around the sun.　地球は太陽の周囲を回る。（不変の真理）
> 2　I get up at 6:30 every morning.　私は毎朝6時半に起きる。（習慣）
> 3　Carpenters build houses.　大工は家を建てる。（客観的記述）

② 過去形

過去形は、過去に起きたことや状態を表します。たとえば、I got up at 6:30 today.（私は今日6時半に起きた）は過去に起きた動作を表します。

③ 現在進行形

現在進行形は、現在継続している事柄を表します。Carpenters build houses. のような現在形であれば、客観的記述ですが、Carpenters are building a house.（大工たちが家を建て

ている）のような現在進行形であれば、現在行われている動作を表します。

④ **過去進行形**

過去進行形は、ある過去の時点で行われていた事柄を表します。

> × I watched television when you called me.
> ○ I was watching television when you called me.

　上の文は「あなたが電話をかけるときにはいつも私はテレビを見ていた」という不自然な意味になります。「あなたが電話をかけたとき、私は（実際に）テレビを見ていた」ということを表現するためには、下の文のように過去進行形を用いなければなりません。

Exercise 1　空所に入れるのに最も適当なものを選んで文を完成させなさい。

(1)　I was taught at school that the earth (　　) around the sun.
(a) goes　(b) went　(c) has gone　(d) had gone

(2)　Richard's family (　　) in Chicago from 1980 to 1987, and then moved to Los Angeles.
(a) lived　(b) have lived　(c) has been living　(d) are living

(3)　I (　　) English intensively for five hours yesterday.
(a) studied　(b) have studied　(c) have been studying　(d) had been studying

(4)　The inventor of dynamite was Alfred Nobel, who also (　　) the Nobel Prize.
(a) establishes　(b) established　(c) establishing　(d) was establishing

(5)　Be quiet, please. I (　　) on the telephone.
(a) speak　(b) talk　(c) am talking　(d) was speaking

(6)　When it began to get dark, the boys (　　) outside.
(a) are playing　(b) had played　(c) have played　(d) were playing

(7)　One of my friends (　　) a newly released computer game.
(a) has　(b) have　(c) is having　(d) are having

(8)　Takashi is now in San Francisco. He (　　) at the Palace Hotel. He usually stays at the Palace Hotel when he is in San Francisco.
(a) stays　(b) is staying　(c) stayed　(d) was staying

(9)　We (　　) to a famous museum in Boston next year.
(a) are thinking to go　(b) think of going　(c) think to go　(d) are thinking of going

(10)　She is alive! She (　　), but that young man saved her, just in time.

(a) was drowning　(b) drowned　(c) is drowning　(d) has drowned

3-2　完了形

完了形には、**現在完了、過去完了、未来完了**があります。完了形の基本の意味は、**完了、継続、経験**の3つです。

① 現在完了

> 1　Things in town have completely changed.
> 　　街の様子はすっかり変わった。(完了)
> 2　I have known her for ten years.
> 　　私は10年前から彼女のことを知っている。(継続)
> 3　I have been to the United States three times.
> 　　私は合衆国に3回行ったことがある。(経験)

完了とは、現在より前の時点で、ある事柄が終わり、現在でもその時と同じ状態にあることを意味します。継続は、現在まである事柄が続いていることを表します。経験とは、現在までにある事柄が自分の身に起こったことに言及します。

この中で、過去形との区別がわかりにくいのが、完了を表す現在完了形です。

> 4　I cleaned the shoes.　私は靴を磨いた。(過去)
> 5　I have cleaned the shoes.　私は靴を磨いた。(現在完了)

この2つの文の意味の違いを考えてみましょう。

どちらも過去の時点で「私は靴を磨いた」のですが、過去形を使った4ではその後のことはわかりません。その後、雨の中外に出てぬかるみを歩き、今靴は汚れているかもしれません。これに対して現在完了形を使った5では、今も靴は磨いた直後と同じきれいな状態にあることがわかります。

なお、現在完了は過去のある一点を表す副詞(句・節)と一緒に用いることはできません。現在完了とともに用いることができない語句は、yesterday (昨日)、two days ago (2日前)、just now (たった今)、疑問副詞の when、副詞節を導入する接続詞 when などです。

> × Our meeting has lasted for five hours yesterday.
> ○ Our meeting lasted for five hours yesterday.
> 　　昨日私たちの会合は5時間続いた。

また、「〜して以来」という意味の接続詞や「それ以来」という意味の副詞として働く since は、完了形とともに用いられるのが原則です。

× Liz got a new view of the world since she read the book.
○ Liz has got a new view of the world since she read the book.
　リズはその本を読んでから、新しい世界観を持つようになっている。

　動作動詞を使って継続の意味を表したい場合には、現在完了進行形を用います。

6　The police have been intensively investigating the case for two months.
　　警察はその事件を 2 か月前から集中的に捜査している。

　ただし、動作動詞であっても、毎日繰り返されることに関しては、単なる現在完了形で継続の意味を表すことができます。

7　Bob has worked at the plant for 20 years.　ボブはその工場で 20 年間働いている。

② 過去完了

　過去完了では、基準となる時点がそれぞれ過去の時点に移動するだけです。また、過去完了には単純に過去より古いことを表す「大過去」という用法があります。

1　It had stopped snowing when I woke up.
　　私が起きたときには雪はやんでいた。（過去の時点での完了）
2　Meg's parents had been married for three years when she was born.
　　両親が結婚してから 3 年経ってメグが生まれた。（過去の時点までの継続）
3　The alpinist had climbed Mt McKinley three times when he joined the party.
　　その登山家は、そのパーティに参加したときには、マッキンリー山にもう 3 度も登っていた。（過去の時点までの経験）
4　The man said that he had witnessed the scene of the crime.
　　その男は、自分がその犯罪の現場を目撃したと言った。（大過去）

　なお 4 では that 節の中は必ずしも過去完了である必要はなく、過去形で表現してもかまいません。

The man said that he witnessed the scene of the crime.

③ 未来完了

　未来完了では、基準となる時点が未来の時点に移動するだけです。なお、未来完了では 1 人称主語の場合にまれに shall が用いられることがあります。

1　These kinds of ideas will have faded out in 30 years.
　　こういった考えは 30 年後には姿を消しているだろう。（未来の時点までの完了）
2　We will have been married for ten years next June.
　　次の 7 月で私たちが結婚してから 10 年になる。（未来の時点までの継続）

3   I will have failed the driving test five times if I do it again.
今度失敗したら、運転免許の試験に5回失敗したことになる。（未来の時点までの経験）

Exercise 2　空所に入れるのに最も適当なものを選んで文を完成させなさい。

(1)　Surely, the train (　　) the station; there is nobody on the platform.
(a) has left　(b) leaves　(c) has started　(d) starting

(2)　The earth has (　　) for more than four billion years.
(a) appeared　(b) existed　(c) occurred　(d) proceeded

(3)　She is tired of her husband's jokes because she (　　) them so many times before.
(a) was hearing　(b) have heard　(c) hears　(d) has heard

(4)　The plane leaves at 6:00 and Kevin (　　) at the airport yet.
(a) doesn't arrive　(b) hasn't arrived　(c) won't be arrived　(d) isn't arrived

(5)　When you called on your father last night, (　　) back from his work?
(a) does he come　(b) can he already come
(c) has he come　(d) had he already come

(6)　Her parents (　　) for six years when she was born.
(a) got married　(b) have been married　(c) had been married　(d) married

(7)　She didn't want to go to the movies with us because she (　　) the movie before.
(a) had seen　(b) seen　(c) was seen　(d) will see

(8)　We arrived at home late at night and found that somebody (　　) into the house during the day.
(a) have broken　(b) broke　(c) would break　(d) had broken

(9)　It was my first time on an airplane. I was very nervous because I (　　) before.
(a) have already flown　(b) never fly　(c) did not fly　(d) had not flown

(10)　Akiko always goes to bed at 10 p.m. Tomoko is planning to visit Akiko's house at 10:30 this evening, so when Tomoko arrives, Akiko (　　).
(a) went to bed　(b) has gone to bed
(c) will have gone to bed　(d) had gone to bed

(11)　We (　　) for five years on September 5 this year.
(a) will have been married　(b) will have married
(c) will be married　(d) will marry

(12) I've (　) him since the little fight we had last week.
(a) avoided to talk to　(b) been avoiding
(c) been avoiding in meeting　(d) had avoided

(13) Mary (　) for the company for three years next April.
(a) will have been working　(b) have worked
(c) will work　(d) has been working

(14) When I was a child, I (　) the piano.
(a) was playing　(b) had played　(c) had been playing　(d) played

(15) It has (　) twenty years since my best friend, Miho, and I met in the children's choir.
(a) been　(b) left　(c) passed　(d) taken

(16) Sun Ltd. (　) off twenty percent of the work force since 2001.
(a) will lay　(b) is laying　(c) lays　(d) has laid

3-3　未来時制

　現在の時点よりもあとに起こる事柄を表すための時制が未来時制です。未来を表すためには、will / shall、be going to、進行形の3つを用います。この3つが表す意味は必ずしも同じではないことに注意しましょう。

① will の用法
(a)　単純未来
　未来に起こることが予定されている事柄を表すのが「単純未来」です。

1　Our university festival will be held this coming weekend.
　　私たちの大学祭は今度の週末に行われる。
2　I'll be waiting for you at the gate.
　　私はあなたを入り口のところで待っています。

　1人称主語の場合、単純未来を表す場合は、will be doing という未来進行形を用いるのが普通です。

(b)　現時点における意志、決定

3　"My baggage is awfully heavy." "I'll help you with it."
　　「私の荷物はすごく重いです」「私が持つのを手伝いましょう」
4　I'll go and get the glasses.
　　グラスを取りに行ってきます。

(c) 依頼、勧誘

Will you...? で依頼を表し、Won't you... で勧誘を表します。

> 5　Will you call me later?　あとで電話してください。
> 6　Won't you join us for lunch?　一緒に昼食を食べませんか。

② be going to の用法
(a) 話し手の確信

状況からそのようなことが起きると確信できる場合です。

> 7　It's going to snow before tonight.　今夜までには雪が降りそうだ。

(b) 決定済み

すでに決定している事柄や、前々から考えていた事柄に対して使います。

> 8　We are going to travel to Brazil during our summer vacation. Won't you join us?
> 　　私たちは夏休みの間にブラジルに行くつもりです。一緒に行きませんか。
> 9　What are you going to wear to the party?
> 　　パーティには何を着ていくつもりですか。

今思いついたことについては be going to は用いません。

> (The telephone rings.)
> × I'm going to answer it.
> ○ I'll answer it.
> 　（電話が鳴って）私が出ます。

(c) 予定

be going to はすでに予定されている、あるいは決心した事柄を表せます。とくに人が主語の場合には、これとほぼ同じ意味を現在進行形で表すことができます。

> We are going to visit the art museum tomorrow.
> We are visiting the art museum tomorrow.
> 私たちは明日その美術館に行く予定です。

> Are you going to meet the mayor this afternoon?
> Are you meeting the mayor this afternoon?
> 今日の午後市長に会う予定ですか。

③ shall の用法

shall は現在では、Shall I (we) …? という疑問文で、相手への提案を表す用法で使われるだけなのが普通です。

Shall I turn the air conditioner on?　エアコンをつけましょうか。

Exercise 3　文を完成させるのに、かっこの中から適切なほうを選びなさい。

(1)　(We'll take/We are taking) the 3:30 train. I have our seats reserved.

(2)　"What (will you do / are you doing) next Saturday?" "Nothing. I'm free."

(3)　(They'll leave / They're leaving) Japan tomorrow. Their flight is at 3:30 in the afternoon.

(4)　Do you think Martin (will turn up / is turning up) soon?

(5)　"Why are you putting your make-up on so carefully?" "(I'll see / I'm seeing) my boyfriend."

(6)　Peter can't join us for tennis on Sunday. (He'll work / He's working).

(7)　I'm sure my father (will lend / is lending) me some money. He is generous.

(8)　"Do you have any plans for this weekend?" "(I'll go / I'm going) out with Jill."

Exercise 4　空所に入れるのに最も適当なものを選んで文を完成させなさい。

(1)　I don't have any plans for this Sunday, but next Sunday (　) my aunt.
(a) I visit　(b) I am visiting　(c) I was visiting　(d) I'm going

(2)　(　) this afternoon. I've got my tickets.
(a) I leave　(b) I'll leave　(c) I left　(d) I'm leaving

(3)　(The telephone rings.) It might be Jane. (　) it.
(a) I answer　(b) I'll answer　(c) I'm going to answer　(d) I'm about to answer

(4)　"All these shoes are dirty." "Yes, I know. (　) them."
(a) I clean　(b) I'll clean　(c) I'm cleaning　(d) I'm going to clean

(5)　Look at the dark sky. (　).
(a) It rains　(b) It'll rain　(c) It is raining　(d) It's going to rain

3-4　時制の一致

主節の動詞が過去時制のとき、従属節である that 節の中の動詞の時制は、主動詞の時制

に合わせて過去時制になります。これを「時制の一致」と呼びます。

> 1 He insisted that he was innocent.
>   彼は自分が無実だと言い張った。
> 2 We knew that the invention would cause disaster in the near future.
>   その発明が近い将来に大災害を引き起こすだろうということを私たちは知っていた。

1 では過去において「～だ」と主張した、という意味なので that 節の中の be 動詞が過去形 was になります。2 では that 節の中は過去から見た未来なので、will の過去形の would を使います。

Exercise 5　空所に入れるのに最も適当なものを選んで文を完成させなさい。

(1)　We hoped that the train (　　) on time.
(a) will be　(b) is　(c) did come　(d) would be

(2)　The team of scientists announced that they (　　) in producing a new type of pluripotency cell.
(a) succeed　(b) will succeed　(c) have succeeded　(d) had succeeded

(3)　We all thought that he (　　) a figure in the future.
(a) cuts　(b) will cut　(c) would cut　(d) cut

(4)　She politely asked me if I (　　) carry the suitcase for her.
(a) could　(b) have to　(c) want　(d) shall

(5)　We expected that the construction (　　) completed in a few weeks.
(a) was　(b) will be　(c) would be　(d) had been

Unit 4
助動詞

4-1 助動詞の基礎

① can の用法

(a) 「〜できる」→「〜してよい」

can は「〜できる」という**能力**の意味を表すのが基本です。疑問文の Can I...? は許可を求める場合に用いられ、you can... は「〜してよい」という許可の意味になることがあります。

(b) 「〜できない」→「〜するはずがない」

cannot は「〜できない」「〜するはずがない」という意味になります。

(c) 「〜できた」→「〜できる状態にあった」

can の過去形は could ですが、過去に 1 度起きたことに関して could は使えません。肯定文で could が用いられる場合、「〜できる状態にあった（けれども、できたかどうかはわからない）」という意味になります。また、多くの場合、助動詞の過去形は仮定法で用いられます。

> × I could escape from the fire.
> ○ I escaped from the fire.
> ○ I was able to escape from the fire.
> 　私は火事から逃れることができた。

(d) could

Can you...? で「〜してもらえますか」という依頼の意味を作ります。Could you...? がより丁寧な言い方で、一般的にはこちらを用います。

② 「できる」を意味するその他の助動詞

「〜できる」は be able to do、get to do でも表せます。be able to do は過去に実際に起きたことについても用いられます。get to do は疑問文や否定文でよく用いられます。

> 1　Bob can speak five languages.　ボブは 5 か国語が話せる。
> 2　Can I have a Big Mac, French Fries, and a large Coke?
> 　　ビッグマックとフレンチフライとコーラの大をください。
> 3　What he said cannot be true.　彼が言ったことが本当であるはずはない。
> 4　Could you tell me which bus I should take to go to the municipal office?
> 　　市役所に行くにはどのバスに乗ったらいいか教えていただけませんか。

5 I can't concentrate on studying because you are chatting there.
　君たちがここでおしゃべりをしているので、私は勉強に集中できない。
6 Did you get to see the actress and interview her?
　その女優に会ってインタビューできましたか。

③ may の用法
(a)「～するかもしれない」「～してもよい」
　may は「～するかもしれない」(可能性)、「～してもよい」(許可) という意味を表します。
(b)「～しないかもしれない」「～してはならない」
　may not は「～しないかもしれない」「～してはならない」という意味を表します。may not は「～しないでください」という丁寧な禁止を表すこともあります。
(c) might
　may の過去形は might ですが、may の意味をやわらげる働きをするだけで、過去の事柄を表すことはありません。仮定法の帰結節、あるいは時制の一致で助動詞に過去形が要求される場合に用いられます。

1 If the factory is closed, many subcontractors may go bankrupt.
　もしその工場が閉鎖されたら、たくさんの下請け業者が倒産するだろう。
2 You may use all the facilities in the university.
　あなたは大学のすべての施設を利用することができます。
3 The train may not arrive on time due to the snow.
　雪のせいで、その列車は定刻に到着しないかもしれない。
4 This is a non-smoking flight. You may not smoke in the aisles or the lavatories either.
　このフライトは禁煙です。通路でもお手洗いでもタバコを吸うことはできません。
5 Judging from the look of the sky, it might rain soon.
　空模様から判断すると、間もなく雨が降るかもしれない。

④ must と have to の用法
　must は「～しなければならない」(義務・命令) や「～に違いない」(確信) という意味を表します。must not は「～してはならない」という禁止の意味を表します。義務の表現は have to, have got to でも表しますが、否定文で must not が「～してはならない」という意味であるのに対し、don't have to (haven't got to という否定形はあまり用いられない) は「～しなくともよい」「～する必要はない」という意味になります。
　need to do も「～する必要がある」という意味ですが、否定文で don't need to do と言うと「～する必要はない」「～しなくともよい」のように、don't have to と同じ意味になります。なお、助動詞の need は否定文・疑問文で用いられ「～する必要はない」「～する必要があるか」という意味になりますが、肯定文では用いられません。
　must は個人的な考えを述べる場合に用いられます。個人的な考えではなく、客観性を示

したいという場合は have to を用います。

1 Sue will be absent from school tomorrow. She has to consult a doctor.
スーは明日学校を休む。彼女は医者に行かなければならない。

ここでは She has to consult a doctor. というのは客観的事実ですから、この has to の代わりに must を用いることはできません。なお、must には過去形がありません。過去の意味を表すためには had to を用います。

2 You must obey the order faithfully. 規則には忠実に従わなければならない。
3 You must be nervous now that the exam is approaching.
試験が近づいているから、君は不安になっているに違いない。
4 You mustn't say a thing like that to her face.
彼女に面と向かってそんなことを言ってはいけない。
5 We don't have to turn in our assignments today. 今日宿題を提出する必要はない。
6 The police had to calm down the angry mob.
警察は怒った群衆を鎮めなければならなかった。

⑤ should の用法
(a)「〜すべきだ」「〜したほうがよい」
　should は「〜すべきだ」（義務）、「〜したほうがよい」（忠告）という意味を表します。
(b)「〜のはずだ」
　should は「〜のはずだ」（推量）という意味を表します。
(c)「〜すべきではない」「〜するはずがない」
　should not（＝shouldn't）は「〜すべきではない」（義務）、「〜するはずがない」（推量）などの意味を表します。

⑥ 義務を意味するその他の助動詞
　ought to で should と同じ意味を表します。ought to の否定形は ought not to、疑問文は Ought S to do...? です。疑問文はあまり使われません。

1 You should be punctual. あなたは時間を守るべきだ。
2 The rescue team should arrive there soon since they left two hours ago.
救助隊は2時間前に出たからもうすぐ到着するはずだ。
3 We shouldn't leave the matter in the air.
その問題を放っておくべきではない。
4 You ought not to be indifferent to politics.
政治に無関心でいるべきではない。

Exercise 1　正しいものを選びなさい。両方入る場合もあります。

(1) The exhibits in the museum are fantastic. You (must / have to) go there.

(2) I cannot attend the meeting tomorrow. I (must / have to) make a business trip to Calgary.

(3) You look pale. You (must / have to) see a doctor.

(4) I didn't understand the instruction exactly, so I (must / had to) ask for a detailed explanation.

(5) David is in a hurry. He (must / has to) meet somebody in ten minutes.

(6) You look upset. What's the matter? You (must / have to) tell me.

Exercise 2　空所に入れるのに最も適当なものを選んで文を完成させなさい。

(1) You (　) be a fast worker to have done so much in such a short time.
(a) can (b) must (c) should (d) will

(2) They lock the gate at eleven o'clock. We (　) be late.
(a) don't have to (b) mustn't (c) needn't (d) should

(3) The evidence is clear, seatbelts save lives. I think all drivers and passengers (　) wear them.
(a) could better (b) ought (c) should (d) would better

(4) (　) it be true that he accomplished a feat like that?
(a) Can (b) Had (c) Has (d) Did

(5) "I heard Mr. Ikeda passed away suddenly." "That (　) true. I saw him yesterday."
(a) can't be (b) must be (c) may be (d) won't be

(6) It is a pity that she (　) have to leave Japan.
(a) might (b) is able to (c) ought to (d) can

(7) Mr. Johnson wasn't home when I called, but I (　) contact him at his office.
(a) must (b) ought to (c) was able to (d) could not

(8) Barbara started to run faster and (　) up with him a few minutes later.
(a) can catch (b) can have caught (c) could catch (d) was able to catch

4-2　助動詞の完了形

助動詞の完了形は、「助動詞＋have＋過去分詞（pp）」という形になります。

① should have＋pp と ought to have＋pp

　どちらも「～すべきだった（のにしなかった）」という過去の事柄に対する非難を意味します。should not have＋pp と ought not to have＋pp は「～すべきではなかった（のにした）」という意味を表します。

② must have＋pp

　must have＋pp で「～したに違いない」（過去の推量）を意味します。

③ cannot have＋pp

　cannot have＋pp で「～したはずがない」（過去の推量）を意味します。

④ may have＋pp

　may have＋pp で「～したかもしれない」（過去の推量）を意味します。could have＋pp、might have＋pp でも同じ意味になります。こういった助動詞は完了形と組み合わせることで、過去に起きたことについて今判断を下しているという意味を表します。

1　We should have voted for the other candidate.
　　私たちはもう一方の候補者に投票すべきだった。
2　You ought not to ignore his advice.
　　彼の忠告を無視すべきではありません。
3　Jill must have taken offence at the insult.
　　ジルはその侮辱に対して腹を立てたに違いない。
4　She cannot have translated the document by herself.
　　彼女がその書類を自分で翻訳したはずがない。
5　The witness may have mistaken somebody else for the defendant.
　　証人は他の誰かを被告と見間違えたのかもしれない。

Exercise 3　空所に入れるのに最も適当なものを選んで文を完成させなさい。

(1)　She (　　) the train. It's already 8:30, and she hasn't shown up yet.
(a) may miss　(b) might miss　(c) may have miss　(d) may have missed

(2)　I felt a shiver run through my body. I might (　　) a cold.
(a) be caught　(b) catch　(c) have been caught　(d) have caught

(3)　This composition is too good. Given his poor knowledge of English, he can't (　　) it himself.
(a) be writing　(b) have to write　(c) have written　(d) write

(4)　She got a terrible mark on the exam. So, she (　　) very hard at all.
(a) would have worked　(b) must have worked　(c) will have worked　(d) couldn't have

worked

(5)　Is it possible that his death might not have been accidental? Could he have (　　), Dr. Winkle?
(a) be pushed　(b) be pushing　(c) been pushed　(d) been pushing

(6)　Yesterday, I ran into an old friend of mine. He (　　) my name, for he never mentioned my name when he was talking to me.
(a) should have forgotten　(b) had not forgotten　(c) cannot have forgotten
(d) must have forgotten

(7)　We think the air conditioner (　　) a long time ago.
(a) can have been replaced　(b) may have replaced　(c) should be replaced
(d) should have been replaced

(8)　The car accident was totally his fault. He (　　) not have been driving so fast.
(a) may　(b) should　(c) must　(d) would

(9)　I (　　) have bought envelopes, but I don't remember where I have put them.
(a) cannot　(b) should not　(c) may not　(d) must

(10)　They should have (　　) believe the new program is about saving the poor and offering protection to them. The program will never work.
(a) better being known than　(b) better than to know but　(c) known better than to
(d) not known better but

4-3　過去の習慣を表す used to と would

　used to と would はいずれも「以前は～したものだった」という過去の習慣を表します。used to は「昔はそうだったが今はそうではない」という、現在との対比の意味を含みますが、would にはこの意味はありません。

○ The girl used to put on weird make-up, but she doesn't now.
× The girl would put on weird make-up, but she doesn't now.
　その女の子は以前は変わった化粧をしていたが、今はしていない。

　used to は状態を表す動詞とともに用いますが、would は状態を表す動詞とともに用いることはできません。

○ I used to live in a quiet place in the suburbs of the town.
× I would live in a quiet place in the suburbs of the town.

　would はしばしば often を伴い、「よく～したものだった」という意味を表します。

> 1　My son would often press me to take him to the aquarium.
> 　私の息子は水族館に連れて行ってくれと私によくせがんだものだった。
> 2　We used to stay up late and discuss literature or philosophy.
> 　私たちは以前は遅くまで起きて文学や哲学を議論したものだった。
> 3　There used to be a large swamp in this area.
> 　この辺りには昔大きな沼地があった。

4-5　強意の助動詞 do

語句を強調するためにあえて do を用いる場合があります。

> 1　I did say that I preferred a smoking room.
> 　喫煙席のほうを希望すると確かに言いましたよ。
> 2　She does mean to protest against the boss.
> 　彼女は本当に上司に対して反抗するつもりだ。

Exercise 4　空所に入れるのに最も適当なものを選んで文を完成させなさい。

(1)　I (　) take a flock of sheep to the meadow in the piercing cold of a winter morning.
(a) had　(b) am used to　(c) was　(d) would

(2)　I still can't believe it, but I really (　) see the actor the other day. He was walking right in front of me.
(a) had　(b) did　(c) should　(d) might

(3)　When I was a child, I (　) have a craving for sweets.
(a) used　(b) used to　(c) could　(d) was used to

(4)　The teacher (　) allow us to play pop music, but now he does.
(a) did use to　(b) had used to　(c) used to　(d) never used to

(5)　I suppose this is where our old school building (　) be in my boyhood.
(a) would often　(b) was used to　(c) used to　(d) would use to

4-5　その他覚えておきたい助動詞

覚えておきたい助動詞を含む表現を示します。

① had better

　had better は「〜したほうがよい」と訳されることがありますが、実際には目下の者、あるいは自分に対する強い命令を表します。had better not で「〜しないほうがよい」という

否定の意味になります。

> 1　You had better concentrate on your research.
> 　自分の研究に集中しなさい。

② would rather

would rather は「むしろ〜したい」という意味です。しばしば than を伴います。

> 2　I'd rather die than live in disgrace.
> 　不名誉なままに生きるよりは死んだほうがましだ。
> 3　I'd rather not undergo the operation unless it is absolutely necessary.
> 　どうしても必要だということでなければ、私は手術を受けたくない。

would rather not で「むしろ〜したくない」という否定の意味になります。would sooner...(than) と would as soon... as も同じ意味を表します。

> 4　I'd sooner be honest about my shortcomings than pretend to be something I'm not.
> 　実際の自分とは違うふりをするよりは、自分の欠点をごまかさないほうがよい。

③ might as well

might as well（may as well と言うこともある）は「〜したほうがよい」という意味です。元来は might as well A as B で「B するのは A するようなものだ」「B するくらいなら A するほうがましだ」という比較の表現でしたが、この as B の部分が省略されたものです。

> 5　We might as well stay put to conserve our strength.
> 　私たちは体力を温存するようにじっとしていたほうがいい。
> 6　You might as well throw away the money as lend it to John.
> 　その金をジョンに貸すくらいなら捨てたほうがましだろう。

④ may well「たぶん〜だろう」

may well は「たぶん〜だろう」という may よりも確信が強い状態を表します。さらに確信が強い場合には may very well と言うことがあります。

> 7　You may well notice the difference in quality between the two products.
> 　2 つの製品の間にある質の違いにはたぶん気づくだろう。
> 8　He may very well get upset if you don't accept his offer.
> 　彼の申し出をあなたが受け入れなかったら、彼はきっと当惑するだろう。

⑤ cannot help doing「どうしても〜してしまう」

cannot help doing、cannot but do、cannot help but do で「どうしても〜してしまう、〜

せずにはいられない」という意味を表します。

> 9　The circus clown acted so funnily that I couldn't help laughing.
> サーカスのピエロがとても面白い振る舞いをしたので、私は笑わずにはいられなかった。

Exercise 5　空所に入れるのに最も適当なものを選んで文を完成させなさい。

(1)　The dark clouds threaten rain. I'd rather not (　　) a walk this afternoon.
(a) have　(b) having　(c) had　(d) to have

(2)　You (　　) associate with such a mean guy.
(a) had better not　(b) used to　(c) not had better　(d) did not have better

(3)　Everybody seems to be exhausted. We (　　) call it a day.
(a) would rather not　(b) would as soon　(c) might as well　(d) may well

(4)　I (　　) feeling sympathetic for their predicament.
(a) had better　(b) would rather　(c) may well　(d) cannot help

(5)　Since her son might have been involved in the accident, she (　　) be anxious about him.
(a) would often　(b) may very well　(c) might as well　(d) would rather

Unit 5
名詞、冠詞、代名詞

5-1 名詞の働き
名詞はものや事柄を表す単語です。文の中で名詞は、主として次のような働きをします。

① 動詞の主語
② 動詞の目的語
③ 動詞の補語
④ 前置詞の目的語
⑤ 別の名詞の前に置かれて、その名詞の性質を表す

⑤の例として orange juice（オレンジジュース）、apple orchard（リンゴ園）、girls high-school（女子高校）などがあります。このような働きをする名詞は単数形になるのが普通ですが、上例の girls high-school（＝high-school for girls）のように複数形をとる場合もあります。

★形容詞・副詞の限定語

worth the effort（その努力に値する）は形容詞 worth がその内容を限定する名詞 the effort をとっています。eighteen years old（18歳）では、eighteen years が副詞句として形容詞 old を修飾しています。同様に、three years ago（3年前）で、副詞 ago（以前）をさらに限定しているのが three years です。

Exercise 1 以下の文で名詞を指摘し、その文中での役割を答えなさい。

(1) The current discussion will further consolidate the already close relationships between the two countries.
(2) Our company has been the most trusted supplier of kitchen utensils in the world and is incessantly pursuing better quality.
(3) The wages, savings and any windfall received by a working class woman belonged exclusively to her husband.
(4) John quit the insurance company and established his own insurance agency three years ago.
(5) I've suffered from a terrible headache recently. I'm afraid it may be a sign of a stroke.

5-2 可算名詞と不可算名詞
英語の名詞には数えられる名詞（**可算名詞**）と数えられない名詞（**不可算名詞**）があります。可算名詞は原則として、単独では用いられず、複数形にするか、冠詞などを前に置い

て用いなければなりません。不可算名詞は複数形にはできず、不定冠詞 a / an とともに用いることもできません。

★代表的な不可算名詞
① 固体、液体、気体のような物質を表すもの（物質名詞）
iron「鉄」、copper「銅」、stone「石」、paper「紙」、soap「石けん」、rice「米」、sugar「砂糖」、bread「パン」、butter「バター」、meat「肉」、chicken「鶏肉」、water「水」、milk「牛乳」、coffee「コーヒー」、mud「泥」、air「空気」、fire「炎」

　以下も物質名詞の仲間。money「お金」、furniture「家具」、baggage / luggage「荷物」、trash / garbage「ゴミ」

② 抽象名詞
advice「忠告」、damage「被害」、energy「エネルギー」、equipment「装備、備品」、fiction「虚構」、fun「楽しみ」、happiness「幸福」、harm「損害」、information「情報」、luck「運」、peace「平和」、progress「進歩」、support「支持」、traffic「交通」、weather「天気」、work「仕事」

③ 集合名詞の一部
　元来はある種類の事物全般を表すものでした。clothing（衣類）、jewelry（宝石）、laundry（洗濯物）、machinery（機械）、mail（郵便物）、merchandise（商品）、poetry（詩）、scenery（風景）、stationery（文房具）など、語尾が -ry で終わるものが多い。
（注）　laundry は「クリーニング店」という意味では可算名詞になります。

Exercise 2　以下の英文の下線部で文法的・語法的に誤りがあるものを選びなさい。

(1)　There (a) are furniture in the guest house (b) in the woods and (c) it includes a kitchen table, a large TV, a DVD player and a chest (d) for clothes.

(2)　(a) Airline regulations allowed only (b) two baggages to be carried on (c) board during (d) my flight from New York to Paris.

(3)　We should find (a) more effective (b) ways to make (c) use of solar (d) energies.

(4)　(a) It was (b) a good luck for me (c) to win a ticket to Okinawa because I had made (d) no plans for the summer.

(5)　Educational (a) materials, including academic (b) publications, can be sent at reduced (c) rates as fourth-class (d) mails.

(6)　(a) The telephone, television and the Internet are all (b) communication devices. People use (c) these equipments to make (d) news travel fast.

(7)　Since we don't (a) have many homeworks, let's go out after (b) school and have (c) fun in (d) town.

(8) Kevin told (a) the secretary to put (b) some more papers in (c) the trays of (d) the copier.

5-3 名詞と前置詞の組み合わせ。

　名詞によっては、前後にくる前置詞が決まってくる場合があります。direction（方向）は in the direction で「その方向へ」という意味になります。reason（理由）は for this reason（この理由で）、the reason for our failure（私たちの失敗の理由）のように、for が用いられます。名詞がどの前置詞と組み合わされるのかを確認しましょう。

Exercise 3 　空所に入れるのに最も適当なものを選んで文を完成させなさい。

(1)　I'm sure they have no reason (　　) turning down our offer.
(a) for　(b) in　(c) of　(d) on

(2)　It's not clearly known what the (　　) of the terrible railway accident was.
(a) resource　(b) cause　(c) affect　(d) reason

(3)　There are a wide range of accommodations from back packers to exclusive hotels (　　) the island.
(a) at　(b) by　(c) in　(d) on

(4)　I did not in the least expect to see my name mentioned (　　) the newspaper.
(a) with　(b) in　(c) of　(d) among

(5)　We had nothing to do (　　) the long train trip, so we played cards to kill time.
(a) in　(b) on　(c) with　(d) at

(6)　On seeing us, the deer ran away for her life (　　) the direction of the forest.
(a) to　(b) for　(c) on　(d) in

(7)　He has always had a lot of respect (　　) his boss, enjoyed his job, and contributed to the rise in the profits of the company.
(a) for　(b) in　(c) on　(d) by

5-4　冠　詞

　冠詞には特定のものを表す**定冠詞** the と、不特定のものを表す**不定冠詞** a があります。the は母音の前では [ðɪ] と発音され、不定冠詞は母音の前では an になります。

> 1　He is a doctor.
> 2　He is the doctor.

Unit 5　名詞、冠詞、代名詞　35

1、2とも「彼は医者だ」と訳されますが、1の場合には「彼は医者だ」という、彼の職業を表す働きをするだけです。2はたとえば「私の主治医だ」「私の執刀医だ」「昨日私が見てもらった医者だ」など、彼が自分にとって特定の意味をもつ医者だということを示します。

　3　Dr. Turner is the surgeon who can perform the surgery.
　4　Dr. Turner is a surgeon who can perform the surgery.

　他に条件がなければ、3では、その手術ができる医者はターナー博士しかいない、ということになり、4では他にものその手術ができる医者が複数いて、ターナー博士はその中の1人ということになります。

★ the を伴う名詞の主な用法
① 先に出てきた名詞を受ける名詞

There lived a man in the village. The man had a mysterious power.
その村にある男が住んでいた。その男には神秘的な力があった。

② 聞き手がどれを指しているか理解できる名詞

I'll drop in at the supermarket on my way home.
家に帰る途中でそのスーパーに寄るつもりだ。

　「スーパー」と聞いて、聞き手が具体的にどのスーパーなのか理解できる場合には the を使います。

③ 修飾語句で限定された名詞

I will read the book I bought at the bookstore yesterday.
昨日その本屋で買った本を読むつもりだ。

④ very や only や same や first、最上級の形容詞で修飾された名詞

You are the very woman I've been looking for.
あなたはまさに私が探していた女性だ。

⑤ 唯一物を表す名詞

The sun is shining.　太陽が輝いている。

　the sun（太陽）、the moon（月）、the earth（地球）のように1つしかないものの前には the を置きます。

⑥ 単位、割合を表す名詞

> I'm paid by the month.　私は月単位で給料をもらっている。

the 以外にも、this/that、my/your/our/his/her など名詞が特定のものを表すことを示す語があります。また、a 以外にも、every、some、any、each、another、no など、名詞が不特定のものを表す語があります。これらの語を「限定詞」と呼ぶことにします。

1 つの名詞の限定詞を 2 つ置くことはできません。

× a my friend
○ one of my friends
　「私の友達の 1 人」

× some these people
○ some of these people
　「これらの人々の一部」

the ＋形容詞が「形容詞で表される性質をもつ人たち」の意味を表す場合があります。the rich は「お金持ち」、the young は「若者たち」の意味です。

Exercise 4　以下の英文の下線部の中で、文法的・語法的に間違いがあるものを選びなさい。

(1) (a) Our regulation stipulates that (b) every waiter must wear (c) a bow tie and (d) an uniform.

(2) (a) Birds of (b) the (c) feather flock (d) together.

(3) It is hard to believe that (a) a year and half (b) have passed since (c) the last time (d) our whole family got together.

(4) Let's have (a) a lunch (b) sometime next week when you have (c) a bit more time so we can have (d) a leisurely meal.

(5) (a) Basketball was invented in 1891 by (b) Canadians (c) as the sports which could be played indoors during (d) bitterly cold winter months.

(6) (a) The other kind of person, however, tries to make (b) good friends and explore (c) all the details of life in (d) the another country.

(7) (a) The each person may leave (b) the house when he finishes (c) the assignment (d) due today.

(8) I just noticed that (a) one of (b) the coffee cups you are holding has (c) a stain. Will you hand (d) a cup to me so I can wash it off.

(9) I have never known (a) anybody who bakes (b) pastry as well as you do! Can I have (c) another piece of (d) pie you just served us.

(10) Of course we have to worry about (a) the weather, but it is not (b) only the problem. We also have to take into (c) consideration (d) time left for us.

(11) In Washington, (a) Congress worked overtime to pass (b) a new bill to create (c) more jobs for (d) handicapped.

5-5　another と other, others, some

　another と other は「他のもの」という意味の不定代名詞として用いられる場合と、以下に名詞を伴い「他の〜」という意味を表す形容詞として用いられる場合があります。

(a)　another = an + other → 残りが複数ある中の1つ。
(b)　the other → 2つのもののうち、残りの1つ。
(c)　the others → 残りのものすべて。
(d)　some → 集合体のうちの不定の一部。
(e)　others → 集合体のうち、ある部分を取り除いた残りの一部。

　次の表現を覚えましょう。

・A is one thing, and B is another.「A と B は別だ」
・Some are..., and others are...「…なもの（人）もあれば、…なもの（人）もある」

Exercise 5　空所に入れるのに最も適当なものを選んで文を完成させなさい。

(1)　Would you care for (　　) cup of tea?
(a) another　(b) other　(c) one another　(d) others

(2)　The discovery of the planet Pluto, like (　　) planet, Neptune, was predicted before it was actually observed.
(a) another　(b) one another　(c) other　(d) each other

(3)　Most comets have two kinds of tails, one is made up of dust, (　　) made up of electrically charged particles called plasma.
(a) each other　(b) the other　(c) one another　(d) other ones

(4)　There are four drawers in my desk. One is full of documents and (　) are all empty.
(a) other (b) the ones (c) the other (d) the others

(5)　Can you scientifically reason why some planets have water and (　)?
(a) one does not (b) one other does not (c) others do not (d) some others do

(6)　One of the guests was always telling jokes, but (　) was taciturn and looked more serious.
(a) a few (b) another (c) other (d) others

(7)　He has three siblings: one is a college student, and (　) are office workers.
(a) another (b) other (c) rest (d) the others

(8)　Her reputation is greater than all (　).
(a) the other player's (b) the other players' (c) other player's (d) the players

(9)　To come up with a plan is one thing. To put it into practice is (　).
(a) another (b) other (c) others (d) the other

Unit 6
形容詞と副詞

6-1 形容詞と副詞の基礎

形容詞はものの性質を表す単語で、動詞に後続する補語としての働きと、名詞の前に置かれて名詞を修飾する働きをします。

1　This rooms smells musty.　この部屋はかび臭いにおいがする。
2　It seems inevitable that the company is going bankrupt.
　　その会社が倒産するのは避けられないように見える。
3　We are looking for a creative solution to this problem.
　　私たちはこの問題に対する創造的な解決をさがしている。
4　A famous singer is going to hold a concert in this town.
　　ある有名な歌手がこの町でコンサートを開くことになっている。

副詞は、動詞、形容詞、他の副詞を修飾します。形容詞に -ly をつけて副詞になるものがあります。

5　In the mid-nineteenth century, the world population started to increase rapidly.
　　19世紀の中頃に、世界の人口は急激に増加し始めた。
6　They flatly rejected our proposal.
　　彼らは私たちの提案をきっぱりと拒絶した。
7　The climatic change is a particularly important issue in the world now.
　　気候変動は、今日の世界では特に重要な問題だ。
8　She is much too young for the president's wife.
　　彼女は社長の妻としてはあまりにも若すぎる。

always（いつも）、usually（普通は）、often（しばしば）、sometimes（ときどき）、rarely（めったに～ない）などの頻度を表す副詞は、文中での位置が比較的自由です。通常は、①動詞の前、②助動詞の後ろ、③ be 動詞の後ろに置きますが、④文頭や⑤文末に置かれることもあります。fast（早く）、skillfully（巧みに）、slowly（ゆっくりと）などの様態を表す副詞はさらに位置が自由で、文の末尾に置かれるか、頻度を表す副詞と同じ位置に置かれます。また、文頭に置かれて文全体を修飾することがあります。

9　Students sometimes write compositions without taking grammar into account.
　　学生は、文法を考えに入れずに作文を書くことがある。
10　The boy doesn't clean his room very often.

その少年は、自分の部屋をそれほど頻繁には掃除しない。
11 The sketch renders the scene of the incident <u>exactly</u>.
そのスケッチは事件の場面を正確に表している。
12 I <u>casually</u> made the remark, which triggered a heated discussion.
私は何気なくその発言をしたのだが、それが激しい議論の引き金となった。
13 <u>Fortunately</u>, I secured a room at a hotel conveniently located.
幸いにも、便利な場所にあるホテルノ部屋を確保することができた。

★数量形容詞

「多い」「少ない」を表す形容詞には、可算名詞とともに使われるもの、不可算名詞とともに使われるもの、可算名詞・不可算名詞ともに修飾できるものがあります。

	可算名詞	不可算名詞	両方
多	many, quite a few, not a few, a number of	much, not a little, a great [good / large] amount of, a great [good] deal of	a lot of, lots of, plenty of, an abundance of, heaps of
小	few, a few	little, a lite	

（注1） few, little は「ほとんどない」という意味になり、a few と a little は「少しある」という意味になります。
（注2） 肯定文の単文では many や much はあまり用いられず、a lot of が多く使われます。
（注3） A number of は a small number of で「少数の」、a considerable [significant] number of で「かなりの」、a large number of で「多くの」、a huge [an enormous] number of で「非常に多くの」という意味を表します。
（注4） amount of は a huge amount of や an enormous amount of の形で「莫大な量（数）の〜」という意味を表します。

1 There is <u>little</u> time left to discuss the matter.
その問題を議論する時間はほとんど残っていない。
2 <u>Many</u> students assume that they will be able to graduate from university without studying hard.
熱心に勉強しなくても大学を卒業できるだろうと思っている学生がたくさんいる。
3 Taking too <u>much</u> salt may cause high blood pressure.
食塩をとりすぎると高血圧を引き起こすことがある。
4 <u>Quite a few</u> people must have had the same experience as I have.
たくさんの人々が私がしたのと同じ経験をしたに違いない。
5 Since we have <u>plenty of</u> time, we don't have to hurry.
時間はたっぷりあるので、我々は急ぐ必要はない。
6 The professor is said to give us <u>a great deal of</u> homework.
その教授は大量の宿題を出すと言われている。
7 <u>A huge amount of</u> oil is supposed to be buried in the seabed around here.

Unit 6　形容詞と副詞　41

このあたりの海底には莫大な量の石油が埋蔵されていると考えられている。
8　We had to deal with a lot of problems.
私たちはたくさんの問題に対処しなければならなかった。

Exercise 1　空所に入れるのに最も適当なものを選んで文を完成させなさい。

(1)　These wines should be kept (　　) 7℃.
(a) of a temperature constant of　(b) at a temperature constant of
(c) at a constant temperature of　(d) constant of a temperature in

(2)　I (　　) appreciate your hospitality during my stay at your home last summer.
(a) polite　(b) heartily　(c) hearty　(d) courteous

(3)　The Netherlands is one of the most (　　) populated countries in the world.
(a) dense　(b) densely　(c) deep　(d) deeply

(4)　Many foreign teachers say that Japanese students are usually polite and (　　).
(a) neatly　(b) stiffly　(c) tightly　(d) orderly

(5)　Until about thirty years ago, many professional football players earned very (　　) money. So they had to do other jobs during the week.
(a) no　(b) little　(c) few　(d) enough

(6)　We raised (　　) money at the charity last week.
(a) a lot of　(b) many　(c) any　(d) few

(7)　One of the most frequent complaints among airline passengers is that there is not (　　) legroom.
(a) enough　(b) many　(c) sufficiently　(d) very

(8)　We are going to try that (　　) on the corner this week.
(a) new opening restaurant　(b) newly opened restaurant　(c) restaurant new opened
(d) restaurant of new opening

(9)　Doctors are not sure (　　) a fever.
(a) exactly how disease may cause　(b) how disease may cause exactly
(c) how exactly may cause　(d) exactly disease may cause

(10)　His new apartment was comfortably decorated with (　　).
(a) few furniture　(b) a lot of furniture　(c) many furnitures　(d) several furnitures

6-2 形容詞の基本文型

「It is + 形容詞 + for A to do」という形をとり、「It is + 形容詞 + that...」という形に書き換えられる形容詞に desirable（望ましい）、important（重要な）、inevitable（不可避の）、natural（当然の）、necessary（必要な）、proper（適切な）などがあります。

1　It is important for you to concentrate on study.
2　It is important that you (should) concentrate on study.
あなたは勉強に専念することが重要だ。

これらの形容詞は for のあとに置かれる to 不定詞の意味上の主語を、文全体の主語にする形で文を書き換えられません。

×You are important to concentrate on study.

「It is + 形容詞 + for A to do」という形をとり、原則的に「It is + 形容詞 + that...」という形に書き換えられない形容詞には impossible（不可能な）、easy（容易な）、difficult（難しい）、hard（大変な）、tough（やっかいな）、convenient（便利な）、inconvenient（不便な）、dangerous（危険な）などがあります。

It is easy for her to deceive men.
　×It is easy that she deceives men.
　　彼女が男をだますのは容易だ。

「It is + 形容詞 + of A to do」という形をとる形容詞には、nice（親切な）、kind（親切な）、cruel（残酷な）、careful（注意深い）、careless（不注意な）、clever（頭がいい）、wise（賢い）、sensible（分別のある）、smart（利口な）、absurd（ばかげた）、stupid（愚かな）、foolish（馬鹿な）、silly（愚かな）、brave（勇敢な）、courageous（勇気のある）、cowardly（臆病な）、polite（丁寧な）、rude（不作法な）、naughty（いたずらな）、generous（寛容な）、thoughtful（思慮深い）、considerate（思慮深い）、thoughtless（思慮のない）などがあります。

これらの形容詞は、of のあとに置かれる to 不定詞の意味上の主語を、文全体の主語にする形で書き換えることができます。

It is kind of him to give me a helping hand. = He is kind to give me a helping hand.
彼は親切にも私を手助けしてくれた。

「It is + 形容詞 + that...」という形をとり「It is + 形容詞 + for A to do」という形にならない形容詞には clear（明らかな）、doubtful（疑わしい）、evident（明白な）、obvious（明白な）、probable（起こりそうな）などがあります。

> × It is doubtful for Tom to have tried his best.
> ○ It is doubtful that Tom tried his best.
> トムが全力を尽くしたかどうか疑わしい。

「It is＋形容詞＋that...」という形をとり主語「A is＋形容詞＋to do」に書き換え可能な形容詞には、likely（ありそうな）、unlikely（ありそうもない）、fortunate（幸運な）、unfortunate（不運な）、lucky（幸運な）、certain（確実な）などがあります。

> It's lucky that you are here today.
> ＝ You are lucky to be here today.
> あなたは今日ここにいて幸運だ。

Exercise 2 空所に入れるのに最も適当なものを選んで文を完成させてください。

(1) When (　) to come over here?
(a) are you convenient (b) do you convenient
(c) is it convenient for you (d) does it convenient for you

(2) It would be cruel (　) us to pretend to know nothing about their plight.
(a) at (b) of (c) to (d) with

(3) It is very (　) that there will be snow on New Year's Day.
(a) probable (b) probably (c) probability (d) probabilities

(4) It is very (　) that she will win the first prize in the contest.
(a) maybe (b) certainly (c) perhaps (d) likely

(5) It was rude (　) him to come to the party without being invited.
(a) of (b) at (c) by (d) with

(6) It is common (　) those who make generalizations about the Japanese to compare them to other peoples.
(a) for (b) of (c) to (d) with

(7) Peter smokes and drinks too much. It is (　) that he will have serious health problems in the future unless he starts to take better care of himself.
(a) accurate (b) declined (c) careless (d) inevitable

(8) It was (　) of her to decide not to join in the plot.
(a) sensible (b) sensitive (c) sensual (d) sensory

Exercise 3　以下の英文の下線部で文法的に間違っている箇所を指摘してください。

(1)　Although (a) most of the writings (b) on medicine by the Egyptian woman, Hypatia, (c) have been lost, there are (d) an amount of references to them by other scientists.

(2)　Gandhi was imprisoned (a) for two years. In 1947, however, India (b) was successfully in (c) becoming independent and Gandhi was (d) said to be the most important leader of the country.

(3)　Mahatma Gandhi introduced a (a) policy of non-violent (b) protest which gained (c) many support from the (d) people of India.

(4)　Having (a) little money (b) with me, (c) I am impossible (d) to afford such a costly bag.

(5)　It was (a) very generous (b) for you to (c) lend them your new car (d) for their holiday.

6-3　意味の違いを確認すべき形容詞

同一語から派生して、意味に違いのある形容詞には以下のようなものがあります。

- childlike「子供らしい」／ childish「子供っぽい」
- comparative「比較上の」／ comparable「比較しうる」
- comprehensive「包括的な」／ comprehensible「理解しうる」
- considerable「かなりの」／ considerate「思いやりがある」
- desirable「望ましい」／ desirous「欲している」
- disinterested「公平な」／ uninterested「興味がない」
- economic「経済に関する」／ economical「経済的な、節約家の」
- favorite「お気に入りの」／ favorable「好意的な」
- healthy「健康的な」／ healthful「健康によい」
- industrial「産業の」／ industrious「勤勉な」
- regrettable「残念な」／ regretful「後悔している」
- sensible「賢明な」／ sensitive「敏感な」
- successful「成功した」／ successive「連続的な」
- tolerant「寛容な」／ tolerable「耐えられる」
- imaginable「想像しうる」／ imaginary「想像上の」／ imaginative「想像力に富む」
- literal「文字通りの」／ literary「文学の」／ literate「読み書きできる、博識な」
- respectable「立派な」／ respectful「敬意に満ちた」／ respective「それぞれの」
- valuable「貴重な」／ invaluable「とても貴重な」／ valueless「価値のない」
- priceless「値段がつけられないような」／ pricy「高価な」／ priced「定価のついた」

late と、late から派生した latter、latest、later の違いにも注意が必要です。

- late（補語のとき）「遅れた」、（名詞修飾で）「故〜」

Unit 6　形容詞と副詞　45

・latter「後者（の）」
・latest「最新の」
・later「あとの」
・last「最後の、最近の」

　名詞修飾の形容詞として働く late は the late Dr. Smith（故スミス博士）のような使い方をします。for the last five years（この 5 年間）のような last の使い方にも注意しましょう。また the last person to do / that... で「決して〜しない人だ」という意味になります。

1　He is the last person to break his promise.
2　He is the last person that breaks his promise.
　彼は決して約束を破らない人間だ。

6-4　形容詞と名詞の組み合わせ

　名詞と形容詞を組み合わせて使う場合、日本語からの類推では正しくならないことがあるので注意しなければなりません。

My salary is low / high [×cheap / expensive].
私の給料は安い / 高い。

　cheap、expensive、inexpensive が使われるのは、お金を払って受け取るもの、サービスです。

The book is cheap / expensive.　その本は安い／高い。
The restaurant is cheap / expensive.　そのレストランは安い／高い。

　high / low で高い・安いを表す名詞には charge（料金）、cost（経費）、fare（運賃）、fee（入場料、謝礼）、income（収入）、price（価格）、salary（給料）、wage（賃金）などがあります。

(注1)　income は large / small も可。
(注2)　high / low を使うべき名詞に cheap, expensive を気にせずに使うネイティブも多くいます。
(注3)　amount（数量）、area（面積）、audience（聴衆）、house（家屋）、number（数）、population（人口）、room（部屋）など、面積、体積、量、数を表す名詞は large / small を用います。
The population is large / small [×many / few].　人口が多い／少ない。
The room is large / small [×wide / narrow].　部屋が広い／狭い。
(注4)　The fog is dense / thick [×deep].　霧が濃い。
日本語では、「霧が深い」とも言いますが、deep とは下端から上端までの長さが大きいことを意味するので、霧には当てはまりません。
(注5)　「交通量が多い／少ない」は traffic is heavy / light. と言いますが、much / little を使うこともできます。とりわけ There was little traffic this morning.（今朝は交通量が少ない）のように there is 構文で多く用いられます。
The street is busy.　その道路は往来が多い。

Exercise 4 空所に入れるのに最も適当なものを選んで文を完成させてください。

(1) You should be more ( ) to her feelings.
(a) sensible (b) sensitive (c) sensual (d) sensory

(2) We always try to be ( ) of each other's opinion, no matter how much we disagree.
(a) respective (b) respectful (c) respecting (d) respectable

(3) Have you seen his ( ) movie?
(a) late (b) latest (c) today (d) recently

(4) A ( ) sum of money has been wasted on public construction.
(a) considering (b) considered (c) considerable (d) considerate

(5) ( ) governments have tried in vain to improve bilateral relationships.
(a) Succeed (b) Succeeding (c) Successful (d) Successive

(6) He's been (1) since he was a small child, so I wasn't surprised to hear that he won the (2) award.
1 (a) imaginative (b) imaginary (c) imaginable (d) imagining
2 (a) literal (b) literary (c) literate (d) literacy

(7) ( ) do you think the population of Tokyo is?
(a) How large (b) How much (c) How many (c) What number

(8) I can't believe how ( ) their prices are.
(a) light (b) expensive (c) high (d) few

(9) I arrived here early today because the traffic was ( ) than usual.
(a) busier (b) heavier (c) lighter (d) weaker

(10) We couldn't make out the lighthouse since there was a ( ) fog over the shore.
(a) deep (b) dense (c) thin (d) wide

6-5 接続語句

文と文や段落と段落の間の関係を示す語句が接続語句です。接続語句の働きを理解すると、英語を読んだり書いたりするときに役に立ちます。

① 追加

前の情報にさらに情報を追加するときの接続語句には、and（そして）、moreover（さらに）、in addition（加えて）、additionally（加えて）、furthermore（さらに）、also（そしてまた）、besides（その上）、what is more（さらに）などがあります。

② 対比

　前後の情報を対比する接続語句には、however（けれども）、while（〜なのに）、on the other hand（他方において）、in contrast（対照的に）、in comparison（比較すれば）、but（しかし）、yet（けれども）、nevertheless（にもかかわらず）などがあります。

③ 結果

　前の情報をまとめたり、結論や結果を述べるときの接続語句には、therefore（それゆえに）、for this reason（このため）、this is why（こういうわけで）、consequently（結果的に）、in consequence（結果的に）、as a result（結果的に）、as a consequence（結果的に）、accordingly（従って）、thus（かくして）、so（そういうわけで）、after all（結局）、eventually（結局）、in the end（結局）、at last（とうとう）などがあります。

④ 言い換え

　前の情報を別の言葉で言い換えて説明したりわかりやすくするときの接続語句には、in short（すなわち）、in brief（すなわち）、in other words（言い換えれば）、to put it another way（言い換えれば）などがあります。

⑤ 強意

　主張したいことや強調したいことを述べるための接続語句には、on the contrary（それどころか）、as a matter of fact（実際は）、in fact（実際は）、indeed（本当に）などがあります。

Exercise 5　空所に入れるのに最も適当なものを選んで文を完成させてください。

(1)　The temperature has been rising in recent years. (　　) sales of air conditioners are very high.
(a) Therefore　(b) However　(c) Because　(d) As

(2)　Her sister makes money by playing the violin; (　　), she is a professional musician.
(a) as a result　(b) for example　(c) in other words　(d) on the other hand

(3)　We had been annoyed by noises of one sort or another. (　　) we decided to move out.
(a) In the end　(b) From the end　(c) To the end　(d) On the end

(4)　The doctor told him to keep warm. (　　), he went swimming in the cold lake.
(a) Nevertheless　(b) Although　(c) Moreover　(d) Accordingly

(5)　The trains in Japan are convenient and comfortable; (　　), they almost always run on time.
(a) for example　(b) nevertheless　(c) instead　(d) in addition

Unit 7
態

7-1 受動態の基礎

「XがYを〜する」という通常の意味を表す文を能動態と言います。それに対して、**受動態**とは、能動態の目的語であるYを主語にして「YがXに〜される」という受身の意味を表す文のことです。受動態では、述語動詞が「be動詞＋過去分詞」の形になります。

> Carpenters build houses.　大工は家を建てる。
> 　　S　　　V　　　O
>
> Houses are built by carpenters.　大工によって家が建てられる。
> 　↓　　　↓　　　　↓
> 元の目的語　be＋過去分詞　元の主語

能動態のときの文の主語を受動態で表す場合は、by を使います。

> 1　The area was devastated by the earthquake.　その地域は地震によって破壊された。
> 2　You'll be severely punished if you do a thing like that.
> 　　そんなことをすれば、厳しく罰せられるであろう。
> 3　The team was beaten by the opponent.　そのチームは相手に負かされた。
> 4　They were praised for their good deeds.　彼らは自分たちの良い行いを賞賛された。
> 5　I've been bothered by the traffic noise for the past few weeks.
> 　　私はこの数週間、交通の騒音に悩まされている。

7-2 第4文型、第5文型の受動態

第4文型の Tom gave Mary a book.（トムはメアリーに本をあげた）という文は、第3文型の Tom gave a book to Mary. に書き換えることができます。第4文型の文の受動態は、間接目的語を主語にすると、次のようになります。

Mary was given a book by Tom.　メアリーはトムに本をもらった。

これに対応する第3文型の文の受動態は、直接目的語を主語にし、次のようになります。

A book was given to Mary by Tom.　トムによって本がメアリーに与えられた。

第4文型をもとにした受動文では、能動態で主語だった語句が表現されないことがよくあります。
She gave me this book.　彼女は私に本をくれた。（能動態）

I was given this book.　私は彼女に本をもらった。(受動態1)
This book was given (to) me.　この本が私に渡された。(受動態2)

1　Roy was awarded a special bonus for his achievement.
　　ロイは業績をあげたおかげで特別の賞与をもらった。
2　I was offered the good terms in contract.　私は好都合な契約の条件を提示された。
3　The chef was taught the knack of making his dishes delicious.
　　その料理人は自分の料理をおいしくするこつを教えられた。
4　The land was sold to the real estate company.　その土地は不動産会社に売却された。
5　My message should have been sent to them.　私の伝言は彼らに送られるべきだった。

　　間接目的語が疑問詞の場合には、前置詞を疑問詞の前、または文末に置きます。

× Who was that document handed?
○ To whom was that document handed?
○ Who(m) was that document handed to?
　　その書類は誰に渡されたのですか。

　　第4文型を第3文型に置き換えたときに、前置詞としてtoではなくforを用いる動詞については、能動文の直接目的語を主語にした受動文しか作ることができません。

能動態 My mother made a nice sweater for me.　母は私に素敵なセーターを作ってくれた。
受動態→○A nice sweater was made for me by my mother.
　　　　×I was made a nice sweater by my mother.
　　　　×A nice sweater was made me by my mother.

1　An avocado salad has been ordered for you.
　　アボカドのサラダがあなたのために注文されている。
2　A cup of coffee has been made for you.
　　コーヒー1杯があなたのためにいれてある。

　　ただし、buy「買う」は間接目的語を主語にした受動態を作ることができます。

3　The gorgeous dress was bought for Linda.
　　その豪華なドレスはリンダのために買われた。
4　Linda was bought the gorgeous dress.
　　リンダはその豪華なドレスを買ってもらった。

★第5文型の受動態
　　第5文型の受動態でも能動態の目的語が主語になります。補語はそのまま残ります。

We consider the plan feasible.　私たちはその計画が実行可能だと思う。
　S　　V　　　O　　　　C
　↓

The plan is considered feasible.　その計画は実行可能だとみなされる。

　能動態の O を主語にして the plan is considered とし、その他は能動態と同じままにすれば、The plan is considered feasible. となります。

1　The door must have been unlocked when the burglar broke into the office.
　強盗が事務所に押し入ったとき、ドアには鍵がかけられていなかったに違いない。
2　The plan to construct more nuclear reactors has been rendered unfeasible due to the accident.
　原子力発電所をもっと建設するという計画は、その事故のために実行不可能になった。
3　He has been called a "legend" since he won the ski jump championship in Austria at the age of 41.　彼は41歳の時にオーストリアで開催されたスキージャンプのフライング選手権で勝利して以来、「レジェンド」と言われている。
4　The news has been kept a secret by the government.
　その知らせは政府によって秘密のままにされてきた。

Exercise 1　空所に入れるのに最も適当なものを選んで文を完成させなさい。

(1)　Stomach pains are sometimes (　　) by too much worry.
(a) caught　(b) seemed　(c) affected　(d) caused

(2)　The famous artist was greatly (　　), who wanted him to study art.
(a) influenced by his mother　(b) from his mother's influence　(c) his mother influenced him
(d) influencing for his mother

(3)　The girl has (　　) in the piano by a famous pianist.
(a) given lessons　(b) lessons been given　(c) been given lessons　(d) had given lessons

(4)　While Marilyn was shopping, her five-year-old son (　　) alone at home.
(a) left　(b) is leaving　(c) has left　(d) was left

(5)　The teacher wondered if the main point (　　) clear to all the students.
(a) was making　(b) was made　(c) was made to　(d) made

(6)　What (　　) serve passengers on a plane called?
(a) are the people who　(b) is it that they　(c) language do the people　(d) time do they

(7)　The presentation was (　　) by scientists from major universities all over the nation.

(a) astonished （b）attended （c）attached （d）amazed

(8) It should (　　) that closing the factory is one of the options the company can take to survive the crisis.

(a) note （b）be noting （c）be noted （d）have noted

7-3 受動態において注意すべき事項

受動態の基幹部分（主語＋be＋過去分詞…（by ～））以外は能動態と同じになります。

1　The hotel provided us with the crib.
そのホテルは私たちにベビーベッドを提供してくれた。
→ We were provided with the crib (by the hotel).
私たちは（そのホテルに）ベビーベッドを提供してもらった。
2　The sound made me aware of the incident.　その音は私に事故を気づかせた。
→ I was made aware of the incident by the sound.　私はその音で事故に気づかされた。
3　The teacher caught him cheating in the exam.
その教師は試験中に彼がカンニングをしているところをつかまえた。
→ He was caught cheating in the exam by the teacher.
彼は試験中にカンニングをしているところをその教師につかまえられた。
4　The enemy compelled us to surrender the fort.
敵は我々に要塞を明け渡すことを強制した。
→ We were compelled to surrender the fort (by the enemy).
我々は（敵に）要塞を明け渡すように強制された。
5　We consider the verdict unfair.　私たちはその評決が不当だと思う。
→ The verdict is considered unfair (by us).
その評決は（私たちに）不当だと思われている。

① 受動態進行形

受動態にも進行形があり、「be being＋過去分詞」という形になります。次の２つの文を比べてみましょう。

1　The building is pulled down.
2　The building is being pulled down.

1のような非進行形の文は「その建物が取り壊される」という習慣的な事柄を表します。2のように進行形にすることによって「建物が今取り壊されている」という、今起きていることを表すことができます。また、受動態進行形でも、通常の現在進行形のように確定している未来のことを表すことができます。

1　The matter is being discussed at the conference now.
　　その問題は今議会で議論されている。
2　Cargo was being unloaded from the boat when I passed by the port.
　　私が港を通りかかったとき、積荷が船から降ろされているところだった。
3　You are being deceived by the swindler.　あなたはその詐欺師にだまされている。
4　The hotel was being renovated when I stayed there.
　　私が滞在しているときに、そのホテルは改装中だった。
5　You are being promoted to sales manager soon.
　　あなたは間もなく販売部長に昇進する。

② 受動態で用いられる be 以外の動詞
　動作を表す表現であることを明示するために become / get / grow（〜になる）が、状態を表す表現であることを明示するために feel / lie / remain / stay（〜のままでいる）が、受動態の文で be の代わりに使われることがあります。

1　The non-aggression treaty became ignored when the army invaded our territory.
　　不可侵条約が無視されて、軍隊が我々の領土に侵攻してきた。
2　The pickpocket got caught by the detective when he was trying to pick the woman's pocket.
　　そのすりは、女性からすろうとしていたときに、刑事に逮捕された。
3　Jack grew attached to the town without being aware of it.
　　ジャックは、知らないうちにその町に愛着を感じるようになった。
4　Nobody seemed to want to keep me company, so I felt excluded by everybody.
　　誰も私と一緒にいたがらないように思えて、私はみんなに疎外されているように感じた。

③ 受動態で用いられる by 以外の動詞
　能動態の主語を by 以外の前置詞が用いられる場合もあります。

(a) 主に at をとるもの
be surprised [astonished / amazed / astounded] at A「A に驚く」、be disappointed at A「A に失望する」、be disgusted at A「A を嫌悪する」

(b) 主に in をとるもの
be absorbed in A「A に熱中する」、be interested in A「A に興味を持つ」、be caught in A「A につかまる」、be engaged in A「A に従事する」、be involved in A「A に巻き込まれる」、be lost in A「A に熱中する」

(c) 主に of をとるもの
be convinced of A「A を確信する」、be frightened of A「A を恐れる」、be scared of A「A を恐れる」

(d) 主に to をとるもの

be attached to A「Aに愛情を抱く」、be committed to A「Aに本気で取り組む」、be devoted to A「Aに献身する、Aを熱愛する」、be known to A「Aに知られている」、be restricted to A「Aに限られる」、be married to A「Aと結婚している」、be opposed to A「Aに反対している」、be subjected to A「Aに支配される」「Aを受ける」

(e) 主に with をとるもの

be associated with A「Aと結びつけられる、Aを連想させる」、be covered with A「Aに覆われる」、be involved with A「Aと関わる」、be packed with A「Aを詰め込まれる」、be preoccupied with A「Aに熱中する」、be pleased with A「Aを喜ぶ」、be satisfied with A「Aに満足する」

> 1 We were surprised at her behavior.　私たちは彼女のふるまいに驚いた。
> 2 Tom was so absorbed in the experiment that he didn't hear his name called.
>   トムは実験に没頭していたので、自分の名前が呼ばれるのが聞こえなかった。
> 3 Since we knew his sincere personality, we were convinced of his innocence.
>   私たちは彼の誠実な性格を知っていたので、彼の無実を確信していた。
> 4 Instead of leaving everything to him, we should be committed to the decision-making process.　すべて彼まかせではなくて、私たちは意志決定に本気で取り組むべきだ。
> 5 As far as the eye could reach, the plain was covered with snow.
>   目の届く限り、平野は雪に覆われていた。

④ 再帰動詞（動詞＋oneself）

oneself を目的語にとる再帰動詞が受動態とほぼ同じ意味になることがあります。

・be amused「楽しんでいる」／ amuse oneself「楽しむ」
・be attached to A「Aに愛情を感じている」／ attach oneself to A「Aに愛情を感じる」
・be clothed「着ている」／ clothe oneself「着る」
・be concerned about [for] A「Aを心配している」／ concern oneself about [for] A「Aを心配する」
・be concerned with A「Aと関係している」／ concern oneself with A「Aと関係する」
・be convinced of A「Aを確信している」／ convince oneself of A「Aを確信する」
・be devoted to A「Aに献身している、Aを熱愛している」／ devote oneself to A「Aに献身する、Aを熱愛する」
・be dressed「着ている」／ dress oneself「着る」
・be established「設立される」／ establish oneself「設立される」
・be hurt「ケガをする」／ hurt oneself「ケガをする」
・be reversed「逆転する」／ reverse itself「逆転する」
・be seated「座っている」／ seat oneself「座る」

これらの語句は受動態でも「〜する」という動作を表すことがあります。また be の代わりに get を用いれば、動作であることが明確になります。

> 1　The doctor devoted himself to preventing infectious diseases in the deprived country.
> その医者はその恵まれない国で伝染病を予防することに身を捧げた。
> 2　We concerned ourselves over the effects of thermal power generation on global warming.
> 私たちは地球温暖化に対する火力発電の影響を懸念した。
> 3　The company established itself in 1990 in the wake of the invention of microchips, which make it possible to produce smaller cell phones.　携帯電話を軽量化することを可能にするマイクロチップが発明に続いて、1990年にその会社は設立された。

Exercise 2　空所に入れるのに最も適当なものを選んで文を完成させなさい。

(1)　The new computer system (　　) very soon.
(a) was installing　(b) is being installed　(c) is having installed　(d) installs

(2)　The department store was full of people, and we (　　) farther inside by the crowd.
(a) pushing　(b) was pushed　(c) give a push　(d) got pushed

(3)　I (　　) at Tony's maneuver when he avoided the accident.
(a) amazed　(b) was amazing　(c) was amazed　(d) had amazed

(4)　It's been assumed that life expectancy in the US would rise continuously, but new data suggests that this trend is about to (　　) itself, due to the rapid rise in people who are seriously overweight.
(a) reverse　(b) focus　(c) establish　(d) extend

(5)　It is regrettable that the students aren't (　　) any language classes in order to graduate from the university.
(a) required taking　(b) required to take　(c) requiring to take　(d) to be taken

(6)　My grandfather was (　　) alcohol until his condition had improved enough for him to stop using antibiotics.
(a) forbidden of drinking　(b) forbidden to drink　(c) banned drinking
(d) prohibited drinking

(7)　The reception is slated to start at 2 p.m. and (　　) for three hours.
(a) lasted　(b) last　(c) lasting　(d) have lasted

(8)　Judging from the way he has worked on the project, he is surely (　　) to it.

(a) committed (b) decided (c) associated (d) involved

7-4　句動詞の受動態

「自動詞＋前置詞」「自動詞＋副詞＋前置詞」「他動詞＋副詞」という形の動詞句が1つのまとまった意味を表していれば、その前置詞や副詞を含んだ形で受動態が作れます。

> 1　The police are desperately looking into the murder case.
> 　　警察はその殺人事件を必死に捜査している。
> 　　→ The murder case is desperately being looked into by the police.
> 　　その殺人事件は警察によって必死に捜査されている。
> 2　All the villagers looked up to the minister.　村人は全員その牧師を尊敬していた。
> 　　→ The minister was looked up to by all the villagers.
> 　　その牧師は村人全員に尊敬されていた。
> 3　Kevin didn't know that Ann had taken him in.
> 　　ケビンはアンが自分をだましたことを知らなかった。
> 　　→ Kevin didn't know that he had been taken in by Ann.
> 　　ケビンは自分がアンにだまされたことを知らなかった。

★「動詞＋名詞＋前置詞」の受動態

I made good use of this dictionary.（私はその辞書をうまく利用した）という文からは、次の2つの受動態が作れます。

> 4　This dictionary was made good use of (by me).
> 5　Good use was made of this dictionary.
> 　　この辞書は（私が）うまく利用した。

make use of A の場合、make use of を全体で1つの他動詞とみなせば、A is made used of という受動態が作れます。一方、make use では use が make の目的語になるので、この目的語を主語にした受動態にすれば、use is made of A という形になります。この2番目の受動態は、名詞に何らかの形容詞がついているのが普通です。

> 6　The slight change in her facial expression was taken no notice of by anyone.
> 　　彼女の表情のわずかな変化は、誰にも気づかれなかった。
> 7　The advantage of renewable energy has been made light of.
> 　　再生可能エネルギーの利点はこれまで軽視されてきた。
> 8　No charge was brought against the politician who was rumored to have taken the bribe.
> 　　ワイロを受け取ったという噂のある政治家は、何の告発もされなかった。
> 9　At first little attention was paid to the breakthrough.
> 　　最初はその大発見には全く関心も払われなかった。

7-5　使役動詞、知覚動詞の受動態

使役動詞が受動態で用いられると、能動態で原形で用いられていた動詞は、受動態では to 不定詞になります。

1　No persuasion made me change my mind.
　　どんな説得も私の気持ちを変えることはなかった。
　→ I was made to change my mind by no persuasion.
　　私はどんな説得によっても気持ちを変えさせられることはなかった。
2　Her clothes made her look younger than she really was.
　　彼女の服は、実際よりも彼女を若く見えさせた。
　→ She was made to look younger than she really was by her clothes.
　　彼女は、服によって実際よりも若く見えた。

知覚動詞も同様に、能動態で原形になる動詞は、受動態では to 不定詞になりますが、能動態で用いられる現在分詞は、受動態でもそのままです。

3　The detective observed the man sneak into the warehouse.
　　その刑事は男が倉庫に忍び込むのに気づいた。
　→ The man was observed to sneak into the warehouse by the detective.
　　その男は倉庫に忍び込むのを刑事に気づかれた。
4　The agent heard the people talking about the conspiracy.
　　そのスパイは人々がその陰謀について話しているのを聞いた。
　→ The people were heard talking about the conspiracy.
　　人々はその陰謀について話しているのを聞かれた。

Exercise 3　空所に入れるのに最も適当なものを選んで文を完成させなさい。

(1)　Unknown words should be (　　) in a dictionary.
(a) looked up　(b) checked with　(c) consulted by　(d) discovered from

(2)　This code will never be made sense (　　).
(a) for　(b) of　(c) on　(d) to

(3)　The article is so intricate that it cannot be (　　).
(a) skim　(b) skimming　(c) to skim　(d) skimmed through

(4)　(　　) doesn't seem to be made of these facilities by the students.
(a) Good use　(b) Careful attention　(c) Sufficient notice　(d) Great care

(5)　The vain woman was seen (　　) for bargain goods.
(a) be rushed　(b) rushed　(c) rush　(d) rushing

(6) The company president was made (　) suddenly by the committee members.
(a) resign (b) to resign (c) resigning (d) having resigned.

(7) The thief didn't know that he had been seen (　) into the mansion.
(a) sneak (b) sneaking (c) sneaked (d) to sneaking

(8) The man was seen (　) by the police.
(a) arrest (b) arresting (c) arrested (d) to arrest.

Unit 8
否定・疑問

8-1 さまざまな否定語

否定文は、肯定文に否定語を加えて作られ、「~ではない」「~しない」という意味を表します。最も一般的な否定語は not ですが、他にもさまざまの否定語があります。

① hardly, scarcely, rarely, seldom

hardly / scarcely は「ほとんど~(い)ない」、rarely / seldom は「めったに~(い)ない」。ただし、hardly / scarcely は否定の強めとなることもあります。hardly [scarcely] ... when [before] で「…するやいなや~」という意味を表します。この表現は、しばしば hardly [scarcely] が文頭に置かれ、この場合は主語と（助）動詞の倒置が起こります。no sooner ... than でも同じ意味を表すことができます。

1　I <u>hardly</u> expected that the administration would implement its commitment to improve the pension system.　年金制度を改革するという約束を行政が実行することを私はほとんど期待していなかった。
2　The stubborn man <u>scarcely</u> conceded that he was in the wrong.
　その頑固な男は、自分が間違っていることをなかなか認めようとはしなかった。
3　I had <u>hardly</u> got on the train <u>when</u> it departed.　私が列車に乗るとすぐに出発した。
4　<u>Scarcely</u> had the singer made her appearance <u>when</u> the audience began to applaud her.
　その歌手が登場するやいなや聴衆は拍手を始めた。
5　<u>No sooner</u> had I got out of the airport terminal <u>than</u> I began to smoke.
　空港のターミナルを出るとすぐに、私はタバコをすい始めた。

② no

no は名詞の前に置かれ「~(し)ない」という意味を作ります。no が他の冠詞などとともに用いられることはありません。nobody [no one] は「誰も~しない」、nothing は「何も~(し)ない」という意味になります。nothing は形容詞を伴うことがありますが、形容詞は nothing の後ろに置きます。また none は基本的には「none of +複数名詞」という形で用いられ、複数扱いされることもあります。

1　<u>No</u> sword can penetrate this shield.　どんな剣でもこの盾を貫くことはできない。
2　<u>Nobody</u> anticipated that the average stock price would plummet.
　平均株価が急落することは誰も予期していなかった。
3　There is <u>nothing</u> they can do in order to regain public trust.
　大衆の信頼を取り戻すために彼らができることは何もない。

> 4 None of those methods were satisfactory in their effectiveness.
> それらの方法のどれもが効果という点では満足できるものではなかった。

③ either

　either は否定文を繰り返す場合に用います。なお、either A or B は「A か B のいずれか」という意味です。

> 1　I don't want to change my belief and I can't either.
> 　　私は信念を変えたくはないし、変えることもできない。
> 2　"I won't vote for the candidate." "I won't either."
> 　　「私はその候補者には投票しない」「私もしません」

④ その他の代表的な否定語

　否定文を表す代表的な語句として次のようなものがあります。

・no longer / not any longer / no more / not any more「もはや～しない」
・not either「どちらも～しない」
・neither am I / neither do I / neither was he / neither will she「～もまたない」

　neither は not either と同じ意味を表します。neither [nor] が文頭に置かれると、主語と (助) 動詞の倒置が起きます。Me neither.（私も～ない）という表現が慣用表現として使われます。

・not either A or B / not either A nor B / neither A nor B「A でもなければ B でもない」

> 1　We cannot proceed with the plan any longer.
> 　　我々はその計画をこれ以上続けることはできない。
> 2　The prosecutors didn't believe the testimony the witness gave and neither did the jury.
> 　　検事たちは証人が述べた証言を信用しなかったし、陪審員もそうだった。
> 3　Kate is not sympathetic to them and neither am I.
> 　　ケイトは彼らに同情していないし、私も同情していない。
> 4　I don't want to deal with those people nor do I have time to.
> 　　私はその人たちの相手をしたくないし、そんな時間もない。
> 5　The newly developed laundry machine is neither economical nor environmentally-friendly.
> 　　新しく開発された洗濯機は、経済的でもないし、環境に優しくもない。
> 6　I read both the novels, but I was not impressed by either one.
> 　　私は両方の小説を読んだが、そのどちらにも感動しなかった。
> 7　The speaker was not eloquent nor impressive.
> 　　その講演者は雄弁でもなかったし、印象的でもなかった。

- little [few], if any / if any, little [few]「(ものの存在に関して) あるにせよ、ほとんど何もない」

  if any を強調したい場合は、if any at all と言います。

- seldom [rarely], if ever「(頻度に関して) あるにせよめったにない」
- still less / much less / let alone / never mind「ましてや～ない」
- not in the least / anything but / by no means / far from「決して～ない」

⑤ 否定に近い表現

否定に近い表現として have yet to do、be yet to do、remain to do があります。いずれも「まだ～していない」という意味です。

> 1 There is, if any, little possibility that he will recover from the illness.
> 　彼の病気が治る可能性は、たとえあったとしてもほとんどない。
> 2 There are few, if any, mistakes in this translation.
> 　この翻訳には、たとえあったとしても、間違いがほとんどない。
> 3 Once a pilot is hired, airlines rarely if ever test a pilot for mental health.
> 　パイロットが一度採用されると、航空会社はめったにパイロットの精神的健康の検査を行わない。
> 4 I cannot afford to buy a second-hand car, let alone a brand-new car.
> 　私は、新車はもちろん中古車を買う余裕はない。
> 5 His apology was not in the least sincere.　彼の弁明は全く誠実ではなかった。
> 6 Her dissertation is anything but creative.　彼女の博士論文は全く創造的ではない。
> 7 The dispute has yet to be settled.　議論にはまだ決着がついていない。

Exercise 1　空所に入れるのに最も適当なものを選んで、文を完成させなさい。

(1)　San Diego never gets blizzards and Phoenix (　　).
(a) does as well　(b) does too　(c) doesn't either　(d) nor does

(2)　There is (　　) anyone who is able to solve this math problem in this class.
(a) hardly　(b) narrowly　(c) usually　(d) considerably

(3)　Jacob (　　) hardly left the aquarium when he ran into Jill.
(a) has not　(b) has　(c) had not　(d) had

(4)　We went on a hike to the hill but we had (　　) unpacked the baskets than it began to rain.
(a) no longer　(b) no sooner　(c) almost　(d) hardly

(5)　(　　) figure out how the apparatus worked.

(a) Nobody could (b) Anybody couldn't (c) Nothing could (d) anything couldn't

(6) (　) of us were able to decipher the messy handwriting.
(a) Anyone (b) Everyone (c) Nobody (d) None

(7) I can't attend this boring lecture (　) longer.
(a) any (b) some (c) no (d) either

(8) We couldn't proceed any (　), because the bridge had collapsed.
(a) away more (b) far away (c) farther (d) more ahead

(9) He couldn't make it to the conference, and (　).
(a) couldn't I (b) neither could I (c) not me, too (d) so could I

(10) The man I saw at the scene of the crime was neither tall (　) short.
(a) and (b) but (c) or (d) nor

(11) There was very little room for further discussion, if any at (　).
(a) once (b) what (c) nothing (d) all

(12) Trying to be thrifty, we seldom, (　), dine out.
(a) as if (b) if ever (c) in detail (d) before long

(13) They are not interested in fine arts, (　) in visiting an art museum.
(a) much more (b) less than (c) still more (d) still less

(14) They were not in the (　) anxious about the possible accident of the nuclear power plant.
(a) all (b) last (c) latest (d) least

(15) The role played by the family differs greatly from country to country. In the first place, the definition of the family is (　) universal.
(a) always (b) as yet (c) by no means (d) still

(16) The researchers have arrived at an accurate diagnosis but they (　) how they can cure the disease.
(a) have yet to find (b) have been found (c) have ever found (d) be to find

8-2　注意すべき否定文
① 部分否定
　「全部〜というわけではない」のように、全体のうちの一部を否定する働きが「部分否定」です。not のあとに「全部」「両方」を意味する every や all や both などがくると、部分否定になります。

> 1　I don't know everything about Claire.
> 　私はクレアについてすべてを知っているわけではない。
> 2　Though Brad is an outstanding doctor, he cannot diagnose every disease.
> 　ブラッドは傑出した医者だが、すべての病気を診断できるわけではない。
> 3　Even if you pursue me with so many questions, I cannot answer all of them.
> 　そんなにたくさんの質問を次々に出されても、私はそのすべてに答えることはできない。
> 4　I didn't neglect both my duties.
> 　私は自分の義務を両方とも果たさなかったわけではない。

　not のあとに「必ず」「完全に」のような意味を表す副詞がきても、部分否定を意味します。このように部分否定を作る副詞としては、次のようなものがあります。

- altogether「完全に」
- always「いつも」
- completely「完全に」
- exactly「正確に」
- fully「完全に」
- necessarily「必ず」
- quite「全く」

> 5　We couldn't always come up with original ideas.
> 　私たちはいつも独創的な考えを思いつくことができたわけではなかった。
> 6　We don't exactly agree with your proposal.
> 　私たちはあなたの提案に全く同意しているわけではない。

② 二重否定

　否定語が2つある場合を二重否定と言います。二重否定は、否定が否定されるので、結果として肯定の意味を表すことになります。ただし、二重否定文は単なる肯定文とは異なり、肯定の意味をさらに強調する効果をもちます。

There is no human being who doesn't understand language.

　この文には no と doesn't（＝does not）という2つの否定語があり、二重否定の文です。「言語を理解しない人間はいない＝すべての人間が言語を理解する」という意味を表します。
　このほかに、not A without B「B することなしに A しない」→「A すれば必ず B する」という表現にも注意しましょう。

> 1　If you have a strong will, there is nothing you cannot do.
> 　もし強い意思を持っていれば、できないことはない。

Unit 8　否定・疑問

2　I cannot visit this town without recollecting my childhood.
　　この町を訪れるといつも自分の子供時代を思い出す。
3　Not a day passed without my thinking of you.
　　あなたのことを思わないで1日も過ぎることはなかった（→毎日あなたのことを思っていた）。

③ 否定の強調
　not ～ at all は「全く～ない」という意味になり、at all は否定を強調します。また、at all / whatever / whatsoever は no や not any による否定をさらに強調する働きをします。

1　We have no objection at all.　私たちには全く異議はない。
2　There was nothing strange whatever about the symptoms of the patient.
　　その患者の症状には変わったところは全くなかった。
3　We have not received any complaint whatsoever about the quality of our products.
　　我が社の製品の質について、苦情は全く受けていません。

Exercise 2　空所に入れるのに最も適当なものを選んで文を完成させなさい。

(1)　(　　) turned in the assignment.
(a) All the students didn't　(b) All the students ever　(c) Never all the students
(d) Not all the students

(2)　Not (　　) person can make pottery as skillfully as he does.
(a) every　(b) much　(c) many　(d) a few

(3)　The repairman didn't know (　　) about how to fix this computer.
(a) anyhow　(b) anything　(c) nothing　(d) something

(4)　I cannot read his biography (　　) of the plight of those people.
(a) as to think　(b) in thinking　(c) without thinking　(d) by thinking

(5)　It never occurred to me that he was Japanese because he didn't speak Japanese (　　) all.
(a) on　(b) in　(c) to　(d) at

(6)　They've got no compensation (　　) though they were forced to be displaced due to the accident.
(a) however　(b) whatever　(c) whenever　(d) wherever.

8-3　疑問代名詞

疑問代名詞は「何」「誰」のような、人間やものの正体を相手に尋ねるために使われる言葉です。疑問代名詞には次のようなものがあります。

・who「誰が」
・whom「誰に、誰を」
・what「何が、何を、何に」
・which「（限られた範囲のものの中から）どれが、どれを」
・whose「誰の」

また、疑問代名詞には次のような特徴があります。

(a) 疑問代名詞は文頭に置きます。
(b) 疑問代名詞を用いた疑問文の場合も yes-no 疑問文の場合を同じく、主語と（助）動詞の倒置が起きます。ただし、疑問代名詞が主語として使われている場合には、動詞の位置は肯定文の場合と同じです。
(c) whom の代わりに who が用いられることがよくあります。

1　Who ordered you to command the platoon?
　　誰があなたにその小隊を指揮するように命令したのか。
2　Who(m) will the award go to?　賞は誰がもらうのだろうか。
3　What made you think prices would hike?
　　物価が上がると思ったのはどうしてですか。
4　What in the world are you after?　一体何を求めているのですか。
5　Which is the genuine picture by Picasso?　どれがピカソの本物の絵ですか。
6　Whose proposal shall we adopt?　私たちは誰の提案を採用しようか。

8-4　疑問副詞

疑問副詞は、事柄が起こった時間や場所や理由などを相手に尋ねるために使われる言葉です。また、「how + 形容詞（副詞）」は程度を尋ねる表現で使われます。

・when「いつ」
・where「どこで、どこに」
・why「なぜ」

・how「どのように」
・how much「いくら、どのくらい」
・how many「いくつの」
・how long「（時間・長さが）どれくらい」
・how far「（距離が）どのくらい」

・how often「どのくらいの頻度で」
・how soon「今からどのくらいで」

> 1　When did you decide to adopt the plan?
> いつその計画を採用することに決めたのですか。
> 2　Where is the venue for the annual convention?　年次大会の開催場所はどこですか。
> 3　Why are you eager to study abroad?
> なぜ留学することを熱望しているのですか。
> 4　How can you tell the subtle difference between the two?
> その2つの間にある微妙な違いをどのようにして区別できるのですか。
> 5　How much did you pay for the rubbish, all of which seems to be valueless to me?
> 私には無価値に思えるそのがらくたにあなたはいくら払ったのですか。
> 6　How many doses of antibiotics shall I prepare for the patient?
> その患者には何回分の抗生物質を用意しますか。
> 7　How long will it take my child to realize the truth?
> 私の子供が真実を理解するのにはどれくらいかかるのだろうか。
> 8　How far is it from Earth to Mars?
> 地球から火星まではどれくらい離れているのですか。
> 9　How often do you exchange text messages with Sally?
> サリーと携帯メールのやりとりをどれくらいの頻度で行っているのですか。
> 10　How soon will the inauguration ceremony commence?
> 就任式はあとどれくらいで始まりますか。

8-5　注意すべき疑問詞表現

　疑問詞を使った表現として注意すべきものには次のようなものがあります。

・What if...?　「もし〜だとしたらどうだろう」
・Why don't you / Why not...? / What do you say to...?　「〜するのはどうだろう」

　why not は why don't you の主語と助動詞が省略された表現です。What do you say to の to の後ろには動名詞（動詞の -ing 形）がきます。

・How about...? / What about...?　「〜はどうか」
・How come...?　「なぜ〜なのか」

　how come は文頭に置かれても、主語と（助）動詞の倒置は起きません。そのまま文の先頭に置くだけです。

1 <u>What if</u> you won the lottery?　宝くじに当たったらどうしますか。
2 <u>Why don't you</u> take a break?　休憩したらどうですか。
3 <u>What do you say to</u> replacing all the computers with new ones?
　 コンピュータを全部新しいものと取り替えるのはどうですか。
4 <u>How about</u> weeding today?　今日草取りしようか。
5 <u>How come</u> you object to the suggestion?
　 あなたはどうしてその提案に反対するのですか。

Exercise 3　空所に入れるのに最も適当なものを選んで文を完成させなさい。

(1)　Here's a cell phone, but I can't tell (　　) it is.
(a) why　(b) how　(c) whom　(d) whose

(2)　What is this the blueprint (　　)?
(a) at　(b) of　(c) from　(d) across

(3)　(　　) is this gadget for?
(a) How　(b) What　(c) Where　(d) Why

(4)　Who are we supposed to cooperate (　　)?
(a) together　(b) along　(c) with　(d) to

(5)　What do you (　　) of the idea of consolidating the company?
(a) feel　(b) know　(c) agree　(d) think

(6)　How (　　) did the operation take?
(a) ever　(b) much　(c) long　(d) often

(7)　How (　　) will the balloon burst?
(a) fast　(b) quickly　(c) soon　(d) long

(8)　(　　) miles is a kilometer equivalent to?
(a) How long　(b) How many　(c) How much　(d) What

(9)　Will you please have (　　) coffee ready for the guests?
(a) any　(b) few　(c) little　(d) some

(10)　What (　　) your idea is rejected by the committee?
(a) if　(b) matter　(c) comes　(d) for

(11)　(　　) see an ophthalmologist if your sight blurs?
(a) Why not　(b) What about　(c) Whether or not　(d) How about

Unit 8　否定・疑問　67

(12) What (　) earth were they plotting?
(a) in　(b) on　(c) at　(d) over

(13) "How come you were late for school?"
"(　)"
(a) My father will give me a ride.　(b) My bus got caught in a traffic jam.
(c) School was over.　(d) By bus.

8-6　付加疑問文

付加疑問文とは平叙文の末尾に主語と動詞の倒置形を付加して作られる疑問文です。平叙文を言ってから、その内容を改めて相手に確認するために用いられます。

> You've met her, haven't you?　あなたは彼女に会ったことがありますね。
> He is cool, isn't he?　彼かっこよくない？

付加部分にくる助動詞（be 動詞を含む）は先行する文の動詞・助動詞・be 動詞によって決まります。肯定文に対して付加部分は否定形になり、否定文に対して付加部分は肯定形になります。ただし先行する文が肯定文でも、付加部分が肯定になることもあります。

> You agreed with our proposal, did you?　あなたは私たちの提案に賛成しましたよね。

Let's で始まる文では shall we?、命令文に対しては won't you? または will you? が付加部分に用いられます。

> Let's get to work, shall we?　仕事に取りかかりましょう。
> Fill in the form, won't you [will you]?　用紙に記入してくださいね。

また、I am で始まる文には aren't I が用いられます。

> I'm doing well, aren't I?　私がんばっているよね。

1　His behavior struck you as strange, didn't it?
　　彼の行動はあなたには奇妙に思えましたよね。
2　She didn't notice us dogging her, did she?
　　私たちがあとをつけているのに彼女は気づかなかったんですよね。
3　You are content with the test result, aren't you?
　　君は試験の結果に満足しているよね。
4　Let's stop complaining and get to work, shall we?
　　文句を言うのはやめて仕事に取りかかろうじゃないか。
5　Stop pulling my leg, will you?　私のことをからかうのはやめてくださいね。

8-7　間接疑問文

間接疑問文とは、疑問詞節が文の主語、補語、目的語のいずれかになっているものを言います。

1. How human beings have evolved is not completely known.
   人類がどのように進化してきたのかは完全にはわかっていない。
2. We wondered why they had turned down our offer.
   彼らが私たちの申し出をどうして断ったのか、私たちは不思議に思った。
3. The problem is how we should deal with those picky customers.
   問題は、そういう面倒な顧客にどのように対処すればいいかということだ。
4. It remains to be seen where the new cabinet will lead this nation.
   新しい内閣がこの国をどこに導いていくのかはまだ見えてこない。

8-8　挿入句

疑問詞の後ろに do you think / do you believe / do you suppose（思うか）、do you say（言うか）などの表現が挿入されることがあります。

Where do you think he is?　彼がどこにいると思いますか。

この場合 do you think の部分で疑問文だということを表すための倒置が起きているので、以下の部分（he is）では倒置が起きません。なお、do you know（知っているか）は疑問詞の後ろには置かれず、文頭にきます。

×Where do you know he is?
○Do you know where he is?
彼がどこにいるか知っていますか。

where he is は know の目的節になっています。

1. When do you think we can finish this experiment?
   私たちはいつこの実験を終えられると思いますか。
2. Where did you say we are supposed to meet?
   私たちがどこで会うことになっていると言ったんですか。
3. Do you know where we are heading?
   私たちがどこに向かっているか知っていますか。

8-9　疑問文に対する返答に用いる Yes / No

Yes は相手の質問に対して、答えが肯定文で表される場合に用いられ、No は否定文で表される場合に用いられます。

> You weren't at the scene of the crime, were you?　あなたは犯行現場にいませんでしたね。
> Yes, I was.　いいえ、いました。
> No, I wasn't.　はい、いませんでした。

　I was at the scene of the crime（私は犯行現場にいた）が事実である場合にはyesになり、I wasn't at the scene of the crime（私は犯行現場にいなかった）が事実であれば、noになります。日本語では、相手が言った内容と返事が同じ内容の場合に「はい」、違う内容の場合に「いいえ」を使います。英語とは使い方が違うので注意しなければなりません。

> 1　"You aren't indifferent to politics, are you?" "Yes, I am."
> 　「あなたは政治に無関心というわけではないですよね」「いいえ、無関心です」
> 2　"You don't mean to insult me, do you?" "No, I don't."
> 　「私のことを侮辱するつもりではないでしょうね」「はい、そんなつもりはありません」

8-10　yes か no の選択に注意すべき疑問文

　mind は「いやだ」「困る」という意味を表す動詞です。

Would you mind if I smoked?

　この文は「タバコを吸ってもかまいませんか」と訳されますが、直訳だと「私がたばこを吸ったら気にしますか」となります。ですから「吸っていいです」は「私はあなたがタバコを吸っても気にしない」という否定になるため No で答え、No, not at all. / No, go ahead. などと言います。

　一方、「吸わないでください」は、「私はあなたがタバコを吸ったら気にする」という肯定になりますから、Yes で答えて、I'm afraid yes. のような返事になります。特に吸ってほしくない場合は、Yes, I mind. のように言います。

> "Would you mind sticking out your tongue?" "No."
> 「舌を出していただけませんか」「はい、いいですよ」

Exercise 4　空所に入れるのに最も適当なものを選んで文を完成させなさい。

(1)　The Golden Gate Bridge is located in San Francisco, (　　) it?
(a) doesn't　(b) isn't　(c) didn't　(d) wasn't

(2)　He is not the coward he was, (　　)?
(a) is he　(b) isn't he　(c) doesn't he　(d) does he?

(3)　Give me a hand with this baggage, (　　)?
(a) won't you　(b) shall we　(c) don't you　(d) do you.

(4) Let's stop worrying about the mistake we made, (   )?
(a) will we (b) don't we (c) are we (d) shall we

(5) I'm junior to you, (   )?
(a) aren't I (b) aren't you (c) do I (d) don't you

(6) How soon (   ) resume the lecture?
(a) did he say he would (b) did he say would (c) he said he would (d) he said would he

(7) Who do you think (   ) the most suitable for this position?
(a) being (b) he is (c) is (d) that is

(8) How (   ) my living is none of your business.
(a) I earn (b) do I earn (c) did I earn (d) am I earning

Unit 9
準動詞 1

9-1　分　詞

　分詞は動詞をもとに作られますが、形容詞と同様に、名詞を修飾したり、文中の補語になったりします。現在分詞は元の動詞の能動の意味を形容詞的に使いたい場合に用いられ、過去分詞はもとの動詞の受動の意味を形容詞的に使いたい場合に用いられます。

　excite（興奮させる）のようにもともとの意味が「（人）を～させる」という意味の現在分詞は、「～させる」という意味を持ち、過去分詞は「～する」という意味を持ちます。exciting は「（ものが）人を興奮させる」という意味、excited は「（人がもので）興奮している」という意味になります。

　また、1語で名詞を修飾する場合には名詞の前に置き、分詞で始まる複数の語で名詞を修飾する場合には名詞の後ろに置きます。

1　The spectators were excited at the unexpected result of the game.
　　観客は、予期しなかった試合の結果に興奮していた。
2　The spectators were absorbed in the exciting game.
　　観客は、その刺激的な試合に熱中していた。
3　The movie was so boring that I fell asleep halfway.
　　その映画はとても退屈だったので私は途中で眠ってしまった。
4　The injured people were rushed to the hospital.
　　怪我をした人たちは病院に急送された。
5　It is sometimes dangerous to let an injured person craving for water drink as much as he wants to.　水をとてもほしがっている怪我人に、好きなだけ水を飲ませることは、時に危険な場合がある。
6　We need to raise funds required to realize the plan.
　　その計画を実現させるのに必要な資金を集める必要がある。

9-2　動名詞

　動名詞は現在分詞と同じく「動詞+ ing」という形ですが、現在分詞が形容詞と同様に使われるのに対し、動名詞は動詞の主語、目的語、補語、前置詞の目的語など、名詞と同じ使われ方をします。

1　Owing to word-processor popularization, many people have come to think that writing by hand is troublesome.
　　ワープロが普及したため、手書きが面倒だと考える人が多くなった。

> 2 The flight was obliged to postpone taking-off because of poor visibility.
> 　視界が悪かったので、そのフライトは離陸を延期しなければならなくなった。
> 3 My usual way of spending my free time is strolling in the town.
> 　私がふだん暇な時間を過ごす方法は、町を散歩することだ。
> 4 A lot of people opposed changing the plan for building the network infrastructure.
> 　ネットワークインフラを構築する計画を変更することに多くの人が反対した。

9-3　分詞構文

　分詞構文とは、現在分詞や過去分詞が、副詞節と同様の、時、条件、理由などの意味を表す表現です。

As he felt insulted, he didn't accept the offer.
　　↓
　　Feeling insulted, he didn't accept the offer.
　　侮辱されたと感じたので、彼はその申し出に応じなかった。（理由）

Though I admit the plan is not impossible, I still think it is impractical.
　　↓
　　Admitting the plan is not impossible, I still think it is impractical.
　　その計画は不可能ではないことを認めるが、それでもそれは非現実的だと思う。（譲歩）

　次の例は、分詞構文が「付帯状況」を表す場合です。付帯状況とは、主節が表す事柄と同時に起こっている事柄を表すものです。

Alice said good-bye, waving her hand.　アリスは手を振りながら、さようならと言った。

　主節に後続する分詞構文が、主節のあとに起こる事柄を表すこともあります。

The train leaves Sannomiya at 11:00 and arrives at Umeda at 11:30.
　　　　　　　　　　　　↓
　　The train leaves Sannomiya at 11:00, arriving at Umeda at 11:30.
　　電車は 11 時に三ノ宮を出て、11 時半に梅田に着く。

　分詞構文を否定する場合は、否定語 not, never, hardly などは分詞の前に置きます。分詞構文を完了形にする場合には、「having + 過去分詞」という形にします。完了形以上の過去分詞を用いた分詞構文は、受動の意味を表します。

When he was left to himself, the child began to cry.
　　↓
　　Left to himself, the child began to cry.
　　1 人で放置されると、その子は泣き始めた。

分詞構文の主語と主節の主語が異なる場合、分詞構文の主語が表現されます。このような分詞構文を独立分詞構文と言います。

It being fine, we went on a hike. = As it was fine, we went on a hike.
天気がよかったので、私たちはハイキングに行った。

1 <u>Turning right at the intersection</u>, you'll find the headquarters of the company on your left.
交差点を右に曲がると、左側にその会社の本社があります。
2 <u>Indulging myself in idle speculation</u>, I missed the point of the argument.
無駄な考えに没頭していたので、私は議論の要点を逃してしまった。
3 Princess Diana was often pictured with her legs crossed at the knee, <u>proving even royal conventions change</u>.　ダイアナ妃はひざの上に足を組んだ姿をよく写真に撮られているが、そのことは王室の慣習ですら変化することを実証した。
4 The Yangtze Kiang is the third longest river in the world, <u>running for about 6,300 km across China</u>.
揚子江は世界で3番目に長い川で、6300キロにわたって中国を貫いている。
5 <u>Having pledged to improve the social welfare system</u>, the prime minister couldn't help committing himself to the task.　社会福祉政策を改善すると公約したので、首相はその課題に取り組まざるをえなくなった。
6 <u>Other things being equal</u>, an optimistic person is more suitable for a teacher.
他のことが同じなら、楽天的な人間のほうが教師には向いている。
7 <u>The issue settled</u>, we proceeded to the next agenda.
その問題が片づいたので、我々は次の議題に進んだ。

Exercise 1　空所に入れるのに最も適当なものを選んで文を完成させなさい。

(1)　Automobile manufacturers the world over face (　　) competition.
(a) risen　(b) raise　(c) to rise　(d) rising

(2)　People (　　) crops such as rice, wheat, maize and vegetables are called farmers.
(a) grow　(b) to growing　(c) growing　(d) grown

(3)　We are supposed to send back (　　) reports to the manager.
(a) detail　(b) details　(c) detailing　(d) detailed

(4)　Though the lecture was boring, the students tried to look (　　).
(a) interest　(b) interesting　(c) interested　(d) in interest

(5)　The nurses cared for (　　) soldiers in the fierce battle.

74

(a) wind (b) winding (c) wounded (d) wound

(6) Jennifer founded an organization (　) child adoption.
(a) been concerned with (b) concerned with (c) connected (d) having connected

(7) The problem of the aging population in Japan is getting worse because of the (　) birth rate.
(a) destroying (b) dividing (c) denying (d) declining

(8) Exceeding speed limits and (　) safety belts are two common causes of automobile deaths.
(a) without wearing (b) failing to wear (c) don't wear (d) no being worn

(9) After (　) in the 1880s, the machine was used in hotels and restaurants.
(a) having invented (b) its invented (c) having been invented (d) it inventing

(10) (　) exactly the same routine, he understands my situation better.
(a) Doing (b) Doing as (c) For doing (d) That we are doing

(11) (　) animals the way she does, perhaps Donna should become a veterinarian.
(a) Being like (b) Liked (c) Liking (d) To be like

(12) "We have never been informed about health risks caused by flying," a flight attendant said, (　) "we need to be able to make informed decision."
(a) added (b) to add (c) add (d) adding

(13) During my college years, I would often stay up all night (　) political issues with my roommate.
(a) discuss (b) debating (c) being debated (d) discussing about

(14) We are consuming natural resources, never (　) they will run out some day.
(a) suspect (b) suspected (c) suspecting (d) to suspect

(15) (　) come this far, it would be a real pity to give up this joint project.
(a) Had (b) Have (c) Has (d) Having

(16) (　) by her tutor Ann Sullivan, Helen Keller went on to graduate from Radcliffe College.
(a) Encouraging (b) Encouraged (c) Encourage (d) Encourages

(17) Either asleep or (　), Susan didn't answer the door.
(a) asleep pretending (b) pretend to be asleep
(c) pretended to be asleep (d) pretending to be asleep

(18) There (　　) no available information on the crime, the police asked the mass media for cooperation.
(a) being　(b) in　(c) is　(d) seems

9-4　to 不定詞

to 不定詞は「to ＋動詞の原形」という形の準動詞のことです。名詞、形容詞、副詞としての用法があります。

① to 不定詞の名詞用法

to 不定詞の名詞用法とは、to 不定詞が文の主語、目的語、補語になっているか、形式主語、目的語の具体的内容を表している場合を言います。

> 1　To think is one thing, and to do is another.
> 　　考えることを実行することは別だ。（文の主語）
> 2　My dream as a child was to become an astronaut.
> 　　子供の頃の私の夢は宇宙飛行士になることだった。（動詞の補語）
> 3　Spurred by the referendum, the president decided to annex the area.
> 　　国民投票に後押しされて、大統領はその地域を併合することに決めた。（動詞の目的語）
> 4　With a lot of nations in political discord, it is impossible to make peaceful use of nuclear power.　政治的に争っている国がたくさんあるので、原子力を平和的に利用するのは不可能だ。（形式主語 it の内容）
> 5　Mary found it impossible to continue her studies without a scholarship.
> 　　メアリーは奨学金なしで学業を続けることは不可能だとわかった。（形式目的語 it の内容）

★疑問詞＋to 不定詞

「疑問詞＋to 不定詞」は、名詞としての働きをします。what to do（何をすべきか）、where to go（どこへ行くべきか）、when to start（いつ始めるべきか）、how to do（どのようにすべきか）などがあります。how to do は「～のし方」と訳されることがあります。

> 1　In these days of globalization, one of the issues we now confront is how to improve our communications with people in different countries and cultures.　今日のようにグローバル化が進んだ時代に、我々が直面している問題の1つは、異なった国や文化の人々とのコミュニケーションを改善するためにどのようにしたらよいかということだ。
> 2　Since we didn't receive any directions about when to begin the operation, we didn't know what to do.　いつ作戦を始めるかについての指示を受けなかったので、私たちは何をしたらいいのかわからなかった。
> 3　At first, we couldn't agree on where to put up our tent in the harsh weather.
> 　　最初は、厳しい天候のもとでどこにテントを張るべきかについて意見が一致しなかった。

4　The board of executives seems to hesitate over whether to give a go-ahead to the project.
　　執行役員は、その計画を進める決定をすべきかどうか躊躇しているようだ。

② to 不定詞の形容詞用法
　to 不定詞の形容詞用法とは、to 不定詞が名詞を修飾するものをいいます。

1　Some people doubt whether Columbus was the first European to discover America.
　　コロンブスがアメリカを発見した最初のヨーロッパ人かどうかを疑っている人もいる。
2　Sam didn't have any relatives to rely on when he was in a tight corner.
　　サムはひどく困っているときに頼る親戚がいなかった。
3　There is a tendency for people to lean toward extremes when the economy is stagnant.
　　経済が停滞しているときには、人々が極端に傾く傾向がある。
4　We are looking for a new way to teach English effectively.
　　私たちは英語を効率的に教える新しい方法を探している。

③ to 不定詞の副詞用法
　to 不定詞が副詞として働く場合は、次のような意味を表します。

(a) 目的
(b) 感情の原因
(c) 判断の根拠
(d) 結果
(e) 条件

　結果を表す to 不定詞の副詞用法は、しばしば only を伴います。

1　Global cities are competing with each other to be the most innovative by combining many kinds of intelligence.　世界的な大都市は、たくさんの種類の情報を組み合わせることで、最も革新性をもつようになろうと互いに競っている。(目的)
2　I couldn't prevent tears from falling down my cheeks to see my hometown swallowed by tsunami.　私の故郷が津波に飲み込まれるのを見て、私は頬を涙が流れ落ちるのを止めることができなかった。(感情の原因)
3　Jack must be out of his senses to say such a mean thing to your face.
　　あなたに面と向かってそんなひどいことを言うなんて、ジャックは頭がおかしいに違いない。(判断の根拠)
4　The boy grew up to be a brave soldier.
　　その少年は成長して勇敢な兵士になった。(結果)
5　Kate resisted the temptation only to give way to it.
　　ケイトは誘惑に抵抗しようとしたが、結局は誘惑に負けた。(結果)

6 To be honest with you, I have been suspicious of the man from the beginning.
正直に言うと、その男は最初から疑っていた。(条件)

Exercise 2 与えられた日本語の意味を表す英文を作るように語群の語（句）を並べ替えなさい。なお、文頭の語も、小文字で書き出されています。また指示がある場合はそれに従うこと。

(1) 時間を守ることはビジネスマンの義務の1つである。
(　　　　　　　　　　　　　) of a businessman.
the duties, to, on, of, one, is, time, be

(2) 自分の国を象徴するものを1つ外国の友人に送りたいとき、あなたは何を選びますか。
What (　) (　) (　) (　) (　) to (　) (　) (　) (　) your (　) ?
when, send a gift, foreign friend, you choose, want, do, your country, you, representing, to

(3) 原子力エネルギーを平和利用することは可能だと思います。
I suppose it (　　　　　　　　　　　　) atomic energy.
possible, peaceful, make, of, use, is, to

(4) 珍しい建物があるので、あの通りを歩くのは楽しい。
It's (　　　　　　　　　　　　　　　　).
because of, down, its, pleasant, buildings, that street, unique, walking

(5) 私たちはいかにお客様を満足させるかをいつも優先的に考えてきた。
(　　　　　　　　　　　　　　　　) our first priority.
been, considered, customers, has always, how, to satisfy

(6) 図書館にはおもしろい本がとてもたくさんあったので、私はどの本を選べばよいかわからなかった。
There were so many interesting books in the library (　　　　　　　　　　) choose.
I, which, didn't, to, that, know, book

(7) この彼の絵はまだ不完全です。
This painting (　　　　　　　　　) desired.
of, his, much, to be, leaves

(8) 私はルームメイトを探している。
I am looking (　　　　　　　　　　　).

for, room, share, someone, the, to, with

(9) その国の石油の輸出量は一日あたり200万バレルだ。
The country has （　　　　　　　　　　　　　　　） of oil per day.
barrels, capacity, export, million, the, to, two

(10) チャーチルは、「政治家というものは、明日、来週、来月、そして来年何が起こるかを予見する能力が必要である」と言った。
Churchill said, "A politician needs the （　　　　　　　　　　　　　）
tomorrow, next week, next month, and next year."
happen, going, is, ability to, what, foretell, to

(11) 外国旅行をしていると、私たちの国についてほとんど知らない外国人が多いことに驚くことがあります。
While we are traveling abroad, we are sometimes surprised （　　　　　　　　　）
very little about our country.
are many, that there, foreigners, who know, to find

(12) そんなひどいことを言うとは、アーサーは正気ではなかったに違いない。
Arthur （　　　　　　　　　　　　　　　）.
to, insane, been, a, mean, must, say, thing, have, such

(13) 目を覚ますと、ケイトが私を見つめていた。
（　　　　　　　　　　　　　　　）.
and, at, awoke, find, I, Kate, me, staring, to　一語不要

(14) 彼は、大きくなって有名な科学者になった。
（　　　　　　　　　　　）.
a, be, famous, grew, he, scientist, to, up

(15) 彼は道に迷ったが、さらに悪いことに目が暮れてきた。
First he got （　　）, and then （　　）（　　）（　　）（　　）, it got dark.
lost, make, matters, to, worse

(16) 旅行中はパスポートをなくさないよう細心の注意を払って下さい。
While （　　　　　　　　　　　　　　　）.
traveling, not to, be, your passport, careful, lose

(17) 政府はアジアからの学生が日本でもっと職業に就けるようにするべきだ。
The Japanese government should （　　　　　　　　　　　　） jobs in Japan.
easier, make, for Asian students, to find, it

(18) 私たちの間に秘密などありえない。
It is (impossible for there to be any secrets between us).
any, be, between, for, impossible, secrets, there, to, us

Unit 10
準動詞2・接続詞

10-1 注意すべき準動詞の構文
to 不定詞を使った注意すべき構文としては、次のようなものがあります。

① too ... to ～ 構文「～するには…すぎる」「…すぎて～できない」

② enough ... to ～「～するに十分な…」/ ... enough to ～「～するのに十分に…」
enough は名詞の前に、形容詞・副詞についてはその後ろに置かれます。

③ so as to ～ / in order to ～「～するために」
目的を表します。「so + 形容詞・副詞 + as to」は「～するほど…」「とても…なので～」という意味を表します。

1　The auditorium is too small to accommodate all the students.
その講堂は学生をすべて収容するには小さすぎる。
2　The procedure for filing complaint to the court is too complicated for ordinary people to implement without help from an expert. 裁判所に訴えを起こすための手続きは複雑すぎるので、普通の人々が専門家に助けてもらわないで実行することはできない。
3　The wing of the All Blacks ran too fast for anybody in the Wallabies to catch up.
オールブラックスのウィングはとても速く走ったので、ワラビーズの誰もが追いつくことはできなかった。
4　I don't have enough patience to have you saying a thing like that.
君にそんなことを言わせ続けるほどの忍耐は持ち合わせていない。
5　The teacher's explanation was plain enough for me to understand the formula.
その教師の説明は十分にわかりやすかったので、私はその公式を理解できた。
6　We finished compiling the report quickly enough to make it in the morning paper.
私たちはその報告の編集をすばやく終えたので、朝刊にそれを載せることができた。
7　What should we do in order to reduce greenhouse gas emissions?
温室効果ガスの排出を減らすために、私たちは何をすべきだろうか。
8　The minister was so eloquent as to convert him to a Christian.
その牧師はとても雄弁だったので、彼はキリスト教に改宗してしまった。

10-2　be to do
be to do という形は My dream is to become a pilot.（私の夢はパイロットになることだ）のように、to 不定詞の名詞用法が補語として用いられている場合に加えて、当然、命令、

義務、予定、運命、可能、意志、目的を表すことがあります。この場合の to 不定詞は、形容詞的な働きをしているとみなされます。

1　He is to be pitied rather than to be despised.
　　彼は軽蔑されるべきではなく、憐れまれるべきだ。（当然）
2　You are to get to work right away.
　　あなたはすぐに仕事に取りかかるべきだ。（義務）
3　I was to be promoted to the branch manager.
　　私は支店長に昇進する予定だった。（予定）
4　Since it was before dawn, not a soul was to be seen in the street.
　　夜明け前だったので、街にはひとっこひとり見られなかった。（可能）
5　If you are to get on in life, you have to keep faith.
　　出世したいのであれば、約束を守らなければなりません。（意志）
6　If the new policy is to be supported, we need to publicize it.
　　新政策が支援されるためには、それをよく知ってもらう必要がある。（目的）

10-3　to 不定詞の完了形

　動詞が表す時間よりも前に起こった事柄を表すためには、「to have ＋ 過去分詞」という形をした不定詞の完了形を用います。不定詞の完了形は、seem to do（〜に見える）、be believed to do（〜だと信じられている）、be said to do（〜と言われている）、be likely to do（〜しそうだ）などの表現で用いられます。

1　The man was rumored to have committed a serious crime back home.
　　その男は故郷で重大な犯罪をおかしたと噂されていた。
2　They seem to have been impressed by the lecture of the entrepreneur.
　　彼らはその事業家の講義に感銘を受けたようだ。
3　The spokesman is unlikely to have revealed classified information.
　　そのスポークスマンが機密情報をもらしたようには思えない。

10-4　to の後ろに動名詞が続く表現

　「動詞＋to」のあとに動詞の原形ではなく動名詞が用いられる場合があります。次のようなものです。

・admit to doing「〜したことを認める」
・confessed to doing「〜したことを告白する」
・be confined to doing / confine oneself to doing「〜するにとどめる」
・be dedicated to doing / dedicate oneself to doing / be devoted to doing / devote oneself to doing「〜することに献身する」

- have an objection to doing「～することに反対する」
- be limited to doing「～することにとどめる」
- look forward to doing「～することを楽しみにする」
- object to doing「～することに異議を唱える」
- be restricted to doing「～するにとどめる」
- take to doing「～することになれる、～するのが習慣になる」
- be used to doing「～することに慣れる」
- when it comes to doing「～するということになると」
- with a view to doing「～するつもりで」

> 1 Please confine yourself to making remarks on the matter under discussion.
> 議論されている問題についての発言をするだけにとどめてください。
> 2 They dedicated themselves to developing a unique method of tapping renewable energy.
> 再生可能なエネルギーを利用する新しい方法を開発することに彼らは身を捧げた。
> 3 The employee objected to being laid off.
> その従業員は一時解雇されることに反対した。

10-5 代不定詞

先行する部分の動詞と同じ動詞を使った不定詞を用いる場合、同じ動詞の反復を避けるために to だけを使う場合があります。これを「代不定詞」と呼びます。be 動詞の場合には to be で終わります。

> 1 The company exported the components to the country though they were not supposed to. その会社は、してはいけないことにはなっていたのだが、それらの部品をその国に輸出した。
> 2 You should have stayed put as you were ordered to.
> あなたは言われたようにじっとしているべきでした。

Exercise 1　空所に入れるのに最も適当なものを選んで文を完成させなさい。

(1) The computer is not (　) for the ordinary person in the street to understand.
(a) too difficult a thing　(b) so a difficult thing
(c) such a difficult thing　(d) too a difficult thing

(2) The fire spread (　) fast for anything to be done to extinguish it.
(a) all　(b) enough　(c) so　(d) too

(3) The evidence was (　) for the prosecutor to indict the suspect.
(a) too easy　(b) too many　(c) enough certain　(d) clear enough

(4) Nowadays the average life span is (　) for a person to see many great grandchildren grow up.
(a) enough long　(b) long enough　(c) enough longer　(d) longest enough

(5) The child was so smart (　) the difficult equation.
(a) as to solve　(b) for solving　(c) in order to solve　(d) that it could solve

(6) Because of the air pollution, not a star (　) seen in the sky.
(a) was to be　(b) being　(c) has　(d) had

(7) The elderly man is said (　) an excellent athlete when he was young.
(a) to have been　(b) to be　(c) being　(d) is being

(8) The report was very critical and was clearly (　).
(a) intended　(b) intended for　(c) intended to be　(d) intending to

(9) I have a strong objection (　) treated like that.
(a) to be　(b) whether I am　(c) to being　(d) whether I should be

(10) Singing's influence was not limited to (　) unify meetings in rural black communities.
(a) help　(b) helping　(c) help to　(d) helping with

10-6　副詞節を作る接続詞

　副詞節は時、条件、理由、譲歩などを表します。副詞節の先頭には接続詞を置きます。

① 時を表す接続詞

when「〜したとき」、as「〜したとき」、while「〜している間」、before「〜する前」、after「〜した後」、till / until「〜するまで」、by the time「〜するまでに」、as soon as「〜するやいなや」、the moment / the instant / the minute「〜した瞬間に」、directly / immediately「〜するやいなや」、once「一度〜すると」

② 条件を表す接続詞

if「もし〜ならば」、even if「たとえ〜でも」、unless「もし〜でなければ、〜でない限り」、whether A or B「AであれBであれ」、suppose / supposing「〜だと仮定すれば」、provided / providing「〜という条件で、もし〜ならば」、on condition that「〜という条件で」、in case「万一〜すれば」、as long as「〜である限り」

　時・条件を表す副詞節の中では、未来のことでも助動詞 will は用いられません。

③ 理由を表す接続詞

as「〜なので」、because「〜なので」、since「〜なので」、now (that)「〜なので」

④ 譲歩を表す接続詞

although「～だけれど」、though「～だけれど」、even though「たとえ～であるにせよ」、while / whereas「～の一方で」、grant / granting / granted「～であるにせよ」

1　You should not be seated until you are told to.
　　言われるまでは座ってはいけません。（時）
2　The demand for the linear motor car will have drastically decreased by the time its construction is completed.　リニアモーターカーへの需要は、その建設が完了するまでに劇的に減少しているだろう。（時）
3　Since the consumption tax is going to be raised, we'll need to cut down on our expenditures.
　　消費税が上がることになっているので、支出を減らす必要があるだろう。（理由）
4　We will undertake the job provided you pay us in advance.
　　前払いしてくれるという条件で、私たちはその仕事を引き受ける。（条件）
5　The pension system in this country will collapse unless we accept manual laborers from overseas, and have them pay tax.　もし海外から肉体労働者を受け入れて、彼らに税金を払ってもらうのでなければ、この国の年金制度は崩壊するだろう。（否定の条件）
6　While the economy is developing rapidly in our country, our social welfare systems are still poor.
　　我が国では経済が急速に成長しているのに、福祉制度はまだ貧弱なままだ。（譲歩）
7　The pitcher dislocated his elbow joint the moment he released the ball.
　　そのピッチャーは、球を投げた瞬間に、ひじの関節を外した。（時）
8　No new evidence was spotted though the police raided the house of the suspect.
　　警察は容疑者の家をがさ入れしたが、新しい証拠は見つからなかった。（譲歩）

10-7　同格の that

　名詞の内容を具体的に表す場合、名詞のあとに that で始まる名詞節を続けます。このような場合に用いられる that を「同格の that」と呼びます。日本語に訳すときは「～という」という意味になります。

★同格の that をとる主な名詞

agreement「合意」、announcement「放送、発表」、assumption「仮定」、belief「信念」、claim「主張」、concern「懸念」、conclusion「結論」、demand「要求」、discovery「発見」、explanation「説明」、fact「事実」、fear「恐怖」、feeling「感情」、finding「発見」、idea「考え」、illusion「幻想」、impression「印象」、likelihood「可能性」、news「知らせ」、realization「認識」、recommendation「勧め」、rumor「噂」、saying「ことわざ」、sense「感じ、感触」、statement「声明」、suggestion「提案」、theory「理論」、thought「考え」、word「噂」

動詞が目的語として that をとる場合、その派生名詞は同格の that をとります。

> 1 Rick fell into the illusion that he was almighty.
>   リックは自分が全能だという幻想に陥った。
> 2 We cannot ignore the likelihood that the whole area will become inhabitable.
>   その地域全体が居住できなくなる可能性を私たちは無視することができない。
> 3 Word is getting around that they are getting divorced.
>   彼らが離婚しそうだという噂が広まっている。

Exercise 2　空所に入れるのに最も適当なものを選んで文を完成させなさい。

(1)　I'll be working on my manuscript (　　) dinner is ready.
(a) during　(b) by　(c) until　(d) through

(2)　He's been in hospital for two weeks. That's (　　) he can't participate in this event.
(a) because　(b) how　(c) why　(d) the way

(3)　The little girl held on to her mother's hand and refused to let go of it (　　) they walked through the large crowd of people.
(a) how　(b) that　(c) where　(d) as

(4)　The minute the thief entered the building, the dog (　　).
(a) has barked　(b) began barking　(c) had been barking　(d) is barking

(5)　My family was unable to move to where my father was working (　　) our house remained unsold.
(a) before　(b) during　(c) until　(d) while

(6)　We should help people in need (　　) we are not acquainted with them.
(a) what if　(b) if any　(c) as if　(d) even if

(7)　You must stay put (　　) you are instructed otherwise.
(a) as　(b) though　(c) if　(d) unless

(8)　(　　) at home or at school, parents expect their children to behave themselves.
(a) During　(b) Despite　(c) Whether　(d) Although

(9)　(　　) so many people have applied for the position, it will be difficult for you to be employed.
(a) Due　(b) Why　(c) Since　(d) Despite

(10)　(　　) many states claim to be important in determining who a political party's can-

86

didate for president will be, none but Florida has proven crucial.
(a) When (b) Because (c) Although (d) But

(11) (　) most students want to go to North America or England to study English, Asian countries like Singapore may be another possible option.
(a) While (b) How (c) That (d) So

(12) In this special zone, any corporation can join in the casino business as (　) as it complies with the law.
(a) early (b) far (c) long (d) soon

(13) As far as (　), there's only one solution to the problem.
(a) I think (b) I see (c) I'm sure (d) I'm concerned

(14) In 1808, an English chemist, John Dalton, proposed the theory (　) all matter is made of atoms.
(a) which (b) who (c) what (d) that

(15) They will not sign the shipping contract (　) those conditions are met.
(a) unless (b) without (c) whether (d) despite

Unit 11
関 係 詞

11-1　関係代名詞の基礎

　形容詞ではなく文によって名詞の性質を表す（修飾する）場合、その文のことを「関係節」と呼びます。性質を表される名詞を指し、関係節の先頭に置かれる単語が「関係代名詞」です。

We need a person. The person is suitable for this job.
　　　　　　　　　↓
　　　　　　　　　who
「私たちは人を必要としている」「その人はこの仕事にふさわしい」

　The person は先行する a person と同じなので、これを関係代名詞に置き換えます。the person は人であり、かつ主語なので who に置き換えられます。この who を 2 番目の文の文頭に持ってきます。この例ではもともと文頭にあるので、そのまま who is suitable for this job とし、この関係節を a person の後ろに置けば、関係代名詞でつながれた文ができます。

We need a person who is suitable for this job.
私たちはこの仕事にふさわしい人が必要だ。

　関係節が修飾している名詞を「先行詞」と呼びます。

① 先行詞が人で、関係代名詞が主語→ who
② 先行詞が人で、関係代名詞が目的語→ who（頻度大）/ whom（頻度少・文語的）
③ 先行詞が人以外で、関係代名詞が主語→ which
④ 先行詞が人以外で、関係代名詞が目的語→ which

　that は①から④までのどの場合も使えます。また、②④では関係代名詞を省略することができます。

1　The court decided to acquit the death row inmate who'd been pleading not guilty for a long time.
　裁判所は、長年無罪を訴えてきていた死刑囚を無罪とする決定を出した。
2　We have to come up with a new advertising strategy to appeal to the consumers who [whom] we target for this new product.　この新製品が対象としている消費者に訴えかける新しい広告戦略を私たちは考え出す必要がある。

3　The report said the researcher had used images which very closely resembled ones in her doctoral thesis.　その研究者は自分の博士論文にある画像と酷似している画像を使ったと報告書は述べていた。
4　The precipitation was way over the level which the meteorological agency had anticipated.
降水量は、気象庁が予測していたレベルをはるかに超えるものだった。
5　A politician the public didn't trust at all was appointed to the Chief Cabinet Secretary.
国民が全く信頼していない政治家が、官房長官に任命された。
6　The committee persisted in the explanation nobody in his senses would believe.
分別のある人間なら誰も信じないような説明を委員会は繰り返しつづけた。

11-2　関係代名詞 whose

whose は所有格の関係代名詞です。

The man is suspicious. His English has a strong accent.
　　　　　　　　　　　　↓
　　　　　　　　　　　whose

「その男は疑わしい」「彼の英語には強いなまりがある」

　whose English を2番目の文の先頭に置きます。この場合は最初から文頭にあるので、そのまま whose English has a strong accent とします。これを関係節として the man のあとに置きます。こうして、The man whose English has a strong accent is suspicious.（その英語に強いなまりのある男は疑しい）という文ができます。

1　The article features a young lawyer whose looks have won her a huge internet following.
その記事は、その容貌によりインターネットでものすごい注目を浴びている若い弁護士のことを取り上げている。
2　Synonyms, whose meanings are superficially the same, are not always interchangeable.
表面的には意味が同じである同義語は、いつも交換可能だというわけではない。

11-3　前置詞＋関係代名詞

以下の2文で考えてみましょう。

Kenny was a competent worker. I competed for promotion with the worker.
　　　　　　　　　　　　　　　　　　　　　　　　　　　　　　　↓
　　　　　　　　　　　　　　　　　　　　　　　　　　　　　whom

「ケニーは有能な働き手だった」「私はその働き手と昇進を争った」

whom を関係節の先頭に持ってくると、whom I competed for promotion with となります。この関係節を先行詞 a competent worker の後ろに置きます。こうして、Kenny was a competent worker whom I competed for promotion with.（ケニーは、私が昇進を争っている有能な働き手だった）という文ができます。

whom の代わりに、who / that を用いることもできます。またこの whom はよく省略されます。関係代名詞に置き換えた語の前に前置詞が置かれている場合には、その前置詞と関係代名詞（この場合 with whom）をそのまま関係節の先頭に持ってきて、with whom I competed for promotion とし、これを先行詞の後ろに置くと、Kenny was a competent worker with whom I competed for promotion. という文が作られます。この文では whom の代わりに who や that を用いることはできず、また whom を省略することもできません。

1　She couldn't bring herself to attend the party to which she had been invited.
彼女は招待されたパーティに出席する気にはなれなかった。
2　I couldn't get along with the peer I shared the room in the dormitory with.
寮で一緒の部屋になった仲間とは仲良くなれなかった。
3　A concept can never adequately express the experience it refers to.
概念はそれが表す経験を決して適切には表現することができない。
4　Dr. Manning was an outstanding scholar to whom I couldn't be equal.
マニング博士は、私がとてもかなわない優れた学者だ。
5　The committee I'm a member of is the Event Planning Committee.
私が所属している委員会はイベント計画委員会だ。

11-4 「前置詞＋関係代名詞＋to 不定詞」の形容詞用法

「前置詞＋関係代名詞＋to 不定詞」という形で、関係節と同じように名詞を形容詞的に修飾できます。

1　Will you bring me a knife with which to cut this meat?
この肉を切るナイフを持ってきてくれますか。

a knife with which to cut this meat は a knife to cut this meat with と同じ意味を表します。普通の関係詞節を使えば a knife with which I can cut this meat / a knife (which) I can cut this meat with という表現になります。

2　I'll give you ten minutes in which to solve the problem.
この問題を解くのに10分あげよう。
3　We need to raise funds with which to purchase new equipment.
新しい設備を購入する資金を集める必要がある。

Exercise 1　空所に入れるのに最も適当なものを選んで文を完成させなさい。

(1)　Nowadays suburban shopping centers attract customers (　　) geographically much nearer to downtown.
(a) which is　(b) who live　(c) live　(d) would be

(2)　That was the reason (　　) stopped them from proceeding with the experiment.
(a) which　(b) for　(c) because　(d) why

(3)　The remote hamlet (　　) I visited last summer was an amazing place.
(a) which　(b) what　(c) where　(d) when

(4)　You must not forget all (　　) glitters is not gold.
(a) it　(b) whose　(c) that　(d) what

(5)　(　　) Mom knitted this one, or that one?
(a) Is the sweater　(b) Is there a sweater　(c) Where has　(d) Who has

(6)　She goes to an English conversation school (　　) is high.
(a) whose tuition　(b) which tuition　(c) the tuition of whose　(d) the tuition of that

(7)　I don't know the name of the man (　　) I spoke on the phone.
(a) in which　(b) from which　(c) by whose　(d) to whom

(8)　Zero degrees Celsius (0℃) is the temperature (　　) water changes into ice.
(a) at which　(b) whose　(c) which　(d) on which

(9)　The garage (　　) I keep my car in is just around the corner.
(a) where　(b) which　(c) of which　(d) when

(10)　The paint of the bench (　　) is still wet.
(a) you are sitting　(b) which you are sitting
(c) you are sitting on　(d) on you are sitting

(11)　There are several drawers (　　) we have not searched yet.
(a) which　(b) for which　(c) in which　(d) to which

(12)　We should adjust ourselves to the environment (　　) we find ourselves.
(a) which　(b) at which　(c) for which　(d) in which

(13)　The children need a brighter room (　　).
(a) in that they can study　(b) in which to study
(c) that they study in　(d) where to study

Exercise 2 以下の英文の下線部で、文法的・語法的に間違いがあるものを選びなさい。

(1) Although the reason (a) why they gave in the proposal is plausible, (b) the majority of the delegation thinks that the feasibility of the plan (c) has been (d) called into question.

(2) Did you see the car and (a) the driver (b) who (c) crashed (d) into the house?

(3) When the final game (a) was over, the players thanked (b) the fans in the stadium (c) who support during the game (d) had been fantastic.

(4) As he was (a) driving by, Michael (b) remembered the large park, (c) which his father (d) used to take him on Sundays.

11-5　関係代名詞 what

　関係代名詞 what は先行詞を含んだ関係代名詞で「〜するもの／こと」という意味を表します。多くの場合、the thing which / something that に置き換えることができます。What he said was true. (彼の言ったことは本当だった) では、what he said が「彼が言ったこと」という意味を表し、the thing which he said に置き換えることができます。what は said の目的語になっていると同時に、was の主語としての働きもしています。

> 1　What he said casually caused a heated discussion.
> 　　彼が何気なく言ったことが激しい議論を引き起こした。
> 2　The workers were perplexed by what the president said.
> 　　社長が述べたことに従業員は当惑した。

11-6　関係副詞

　関係副詞とは「前置詞＋関係代名詞」に置き換えることができ、主語や目的語としての働きをしない関係詞です。関係節の中では副詞の働きをします。

　例として He went back to the small town where he was born. (彼は自分が生まれた小さな町に戻った) という文を考えてみましょう。この文は、次の2つの文をもとにして作られています。

He went back to the small town.　He was born in the small town.
　　　　　　　　　　　　　　　　　　　　　　　　↓
　　　　　　　　　　　　　　　　　　　　　　　which

　in which を2番目の文の先頭に持ってきて in which he was born という関係節を作り、これを the small town の後ろに置きます。

　この in which は、関係副詞 where に置き換えることができます。

He went back to the small town in which he was born.
　　　　　　　　　　　　　　　　↓
　　　　　　　　　　　　　　　where

　関係副詞は in which / on which / at which / to which など「前置詞＋関係代名詞」の代わりに用いられます。特に where は、場所を表す名詞を先行詞とするだけでなく、幅広く「前置詞＋関係代名詞」の代わりに用いられます。where のほか、よく使われる関係副詞に when と why があります。また、the way が関係副詞のように使われることがあります。

① **when**
　先行詞が age / time / day / year / period / moment / stage のように、明確に時間を表す名詞である場合、「前置詞＋関係代名詞」が when に置き換えられます。

I remember the day when John first gave me the present.
私はジョンが初めて私にプレゼントをくれた日を覚えている。

　もとになっている文は次の2つです。

I remember the day. John first gave me the present on the day.
　　　　　　　　　　　　　　　　　　　　　　　　　　　　　↓
　　　　　　　　　　　　　　　　　　　　　　　　　　　which
I remember the day on which John gave me the present.
　　　　　　　　　　↓
　　　　　　　　　when

　先行詞が時を表す the day なので、関係副詞 when が用いられます。

② **why**
　the reason を先行詞にとる関係副詞です。

Tell me the reason why you want to quit the job.
あなたが仕事を辞めたい理由を私に教えてください。

　この文は、次の2つの文をもとにして作られています。

Tell me the reason. You want to quit the job for the reason.
　　　　　　　　　　　　　　　　　　　　　　　　　　　↓
　　　　　　　　　　　　　　　　　　　　　　　　　which
Tell me the reason for which you want to quit the job.
　　　　　　　　　　　　↓
　　　　　　　　　　　why

　the reason why はどちらか一方を省略して、the reason または why だけにすることもできます。

Unit 11　関係詞　93

Tell me the reason you want to quit the job.
Tell me why you want to quit the job.

　that を関係副詞として使うこともできます。

Tell me the reason that you want to quit the job.

③ 関係副詞的に使われる the way

I hate the way she criticizes me.　私は彼女の私に対する批判の仕方が嫌いだ。

　この文は、次の2つの文をもとにして作られます。

I hate the way. She criticizes me in the way.
　　　　　　　　　　　↓
　　　　　　　　　　which
I hate the way in which she criticizes me.

　しかし、現代の英語では the way in which という形よりも、the way または how だけで「～する方法」という意味を表すことが多くなっています。

I hate the way she criticizes me.
I hate how she criticizes me.

　ちなみに the way SV は、多くの場合「S の V のし方」と訳されます。たとえば、the way he speaks は「彼の話し方」、the way she expresses her feelings は「彼女の自分の気持ちの表現の仕方」という意味になります。

1　We had to walk on the ground where a lot of landmines were buried.
　　私たちはたくさんの地雷が埋まっている地面を歩かなければならなかった。
2　We first flew to Seoul, where we made the transfer to go to Fiji.
　　私たちはまずソウルに飛んで、そこでフィジーに行くために乗継をした。
3　A growing number of Americans oppose vaccines in an age when most of the contagious diseases seem to have been eradicated.　伝染病のほとんどが根絶されたように思われる時代になったので、ワクチン接種に反対するアメリカ人の数が増えている。
4　The attorney didn't mention the reason why they decided to file the lawsuit against the utility.
　　その電力会社に対する訴訟を起こすことに決めた理由を、その弁護士は言わなかった。
5　Nobody could duplicate the way the female researcher generated the stem cells.
　　その女性の研究者が幹細胞を生成した方法を誰も再現することができなかった。

11-7 連鎖関係節

「Sが～だと言った（思った）XはYだ」という文は、「～であるXがYだ」という内容と「SはXが～だと言った（思った）」という2つの内容が組み合わされたものだと考えることができます。

例としてI bought the dictionary which you said was best.（あなたが一番いいと言った辞書を私は買った）という文を考えてみましょう。この文にはI bought the dictionary which was the best.（私は一番いい辞書を買った）という内容と、you said the dictionary was the best（あなたはその辞書が一番いいと言った）という内容が含まれています。このような内容を持つ関係節を連鎖関係節と言います。連鎖関係節では、主格として使われる関係代名詞も省略されることがあります。

1 One of my subordinates who I believed was trustworthy let me down.
  私が信頼できると信じていた部下の1人が私を裏切った。
2 The Chief Cabinet Secretary didn't hesitate to do what he was convinced was right.
  内閣官房長官は、躊躇せずに自分が正しいと確信していることを行った。
3 Teachers should grope for the potenlial of the students they have decided are not smart.
  教師は、頭がよくないと判断した学生でもその可能性を何とか探してやらなければならない。

11-8 whatever, whoever, whichever

これらの関係詞は「～は何（誰、どれ）でも」という意味を表します。

① whatever

1 The boy believed whatever I said.　その少年は、私が言うことを何でも信じた。
2 I won't change my mind whatever you say.
  あなたが何を言おうが、私は気持ちを変えないだろう。
3 We'll cook eggs in whatever way you like.
  何であれ、お好みの方法で卵を料理します。
4 I won't forgive her whatever excuse she makes.
  彼女がどんな言い訳をしようが、私は彼女を許さないだろう。

上の2と4のwhatever...は、名詞ではなく副詞の働きをしています。この場合には、whateverをno matter whatに置き換えることができます。

2′ I won't change my mind no matter what you say.
4′ I won't forgive her no matter what excuse she makes.

② whoeverとwhichever

whoever / whicheverにはwhateverと同様の使い方があります。

1 Whoever makes effort will be successful.
   誰であれ、努力をするものは成功するだろう。
2 I won't believe the story, whoever tells it to me.
   誰が私にその話をしようが、私は信じることはないであろう。
3 You can take whichever you like.　どちらでもお好きな方を取っていいですよ。
4 It won't make much difference whichever way we take.
   どちらの道を行こうが大差ないであろう。

　whichever は「(2つ以上の限られたものの中から)どれでも」という場合に用いられます。なお、2 の whoever は no matter who に置き換えられますが、1 の whoever は置き換えられません。4 の whichever は no matter which に置き換えられますが、3 の whichever は置き換えられません。

5 It is important to try your best, whatever the consequence is.
   結果がどうであれ、全力を尽くすことが重要だ。
6 Whatever the prophet predicted came true.
   その予言者が予言したことは何でも現実のものとなった。
7 My elbow didn't recover whatever surgery I underwent.
   どんな手術を受けても私のひじは治らなかった。
8 You should seek for whatever future you envision now.
   今思い描いている未来はどんなものでも追求すべきだ。
9 Give this message to whoever is in charge of this facility.
   この伝言を、この施設に責任がある誰にでも渡してください。
10 The negotiation will end up in stalemate, whoever joins in on behalf of us.
   私たちの代わりに誰が加わろうと、その交渉は最後には行きづまるだろう。
11 It's not too much to say that the fate of our company depends on whichever party will win the election.
   選挙に勝利するどの政党も私たちの会社の運命を左右すると言っても過言ではない。
12 Whichever store you do the shopping at, you'll be satisfied with the quality of the products.
   どの店で買い物をしても、商品の質には満足するだろう。

Exercise 3　空所に入れるのに最も適当なものを選んで文を完成させなさい。

(1)　The firefighter had a lot of trouble getting to the street (　　) the houses were on fire.
(a) how　(b) that　(c) where　(d) which

(2)　Would you put back the vacuum cleaner (　　) it belongs?

(a) when (b) where (c) what (d) how

(3)　This is one case (　　) you have to be especially cautious about investing so much money.
(a) which (b) where (c) what (d) how

(4)　Have you yet seen the movie (　　) Brad Pitt is starring?
(a) if (b) what (c) when (d) where

(5)　Enoshima, the place (　　) we first met, remains our favorite spot for summer outings.
(a) at where (b) in which (c) where (d) which

(6)　The 18th century was the period (　　) the Industrial Revolution triggered rapid industrialization.
(a) what (b) which (c) when (d) why

(7)　The reason (　　) I get up early every morning to exercise is that it is still cool at that time of the day.
(a) when (b) how (c) why (d) which

(8)　It is presumed that rules governing the sharing of food influenced (　　) the earliest cultures evolved.
(a) the way in which (b) that the way (c) was the way (d) the way how

(9)　I was just about to sleep (　　) the front-door bell rang.
(a) on which (b) when (c) whenever (d) where

(10)　We saw several people carrying (　　) to be a huge cardboard box.
(a) something like (b) that seemed (c) things looked (d) what appeared

(11)　The man talked to me in (　　) sounded like Arabic.
(a) that (b) what (c) which (d) something

(12)　Everybody wants to stay away from John, (　　) they know is dishonest.
(a) what (b) which (c) who (d) whoever

(13)　More than 40,000 school children live outside South Korea in (　　) experts say is a new era for globalized education.
(a) what (b) which (c) where (d) whose

(14)　(　　), ozone levels in the earth's atmosphere appear to have dropped recently.
(a) However the reason (b) What the reason is
(c) How the reason is (d) Whatever the reason

Unit 11　関係詞　97

(15) We should prepare ourselves to deal with (　) happens.
(a) whoever (b) whatever (c) whenever (d) whomever

(16) (　) has an invitation to this ceremony can join us.
(a) Any people who (b) Whenever (c) Which person (d) Whoever

(17) The manufacturer guarantees that its cosmetic products are good for three years or until the expiration date on the package, (　) is sooner.
(a) what (b) when (c) that (d) whichever

Unit 12
形容詞的修飾語句と副詞的修飾語句

　形容詞は名詞を修飾し、副詞は名詞以外の語句（文、動詞、形容詞、副詞）を修飾します。

12-1　形容詞的修飾語句
　形容詞的に名詞を修飾するものには、形容詞、現在分詞、過去分詞があります。単独では名詞の前に置かれて後ろの名詞を修飾し、他の語と組み合わされてまとまった意味を作る時には名詞の後ろに置き、前の名詞を修飾します。

1　You must use a singular pronoun for a singular noun and a plural pronoun for a plural noun.
　単数名詞の代わりには単数形の代名詞を、複数名詞の代わりには複数形の代名詞を使わなければならない。
2　A rolling stone gathers no moss.
　転がる石には苔がつかない（石の上にも3年。／流れる水は腐らず）。
3　It is no use crying over spilt milk.
　こぼれたミルクのことを嘆いても無駄だ（覆水盆に返らず）。
4　Laser beams can carry long-distance signals in ways somewhat similar to radio waves.
　レーザー光線は、電波と少し似たしくみで長距離の信号を送る。
5　We shouldn't abandon hope however desperate the situation surrounding us seems.
　我々を取り巻く状況がどんなに絶望的に思えようと、我々は希望を捨てるべきではない。
6　Chocolate's varied flavors, colors, and shapes result from different recipe traditions evolved in different parts of the world.　チョコレートが持つさまざまの味わい、色、形は、世界の異なった地域で発達した、いろいろな製造法の伝統に由来するものだ。

　to 不定詞が形容詞的に名詞を修飾することがあります。

7　In response to the oil crises of the 1970's, Japan's large firms introduced schemes to reduce management cost.　1970年代の石油危機への対策として、日本の大企業は経営コストを削減する枠組みを導入した。
8　You picked the wrong person to turn to for advice.
　助言を求めるには間違った人間を選んだね。
9　The hospital did not have the facilities to treat terminally-ill patients.
　末期的な病状の患者を処置する設備がその病院にはなかった。

10 In order to assure safe crossing, the district government has made attempts to reduce automobile traffic.
安全な道路横断を確保するために、地方政府は自動車の交通量を減らす試みをした。

前置詞句が名詞を修飾することがあります。

11 The earth is the only planet with a large amount of oxygen in its atmosphere in the solar system.　太陽系の中では、地球が大気の中に大量の酸素を持つ唯一の惑星だ。
12 The Pueblo appears to be the oldest of all Native American tribes on the American continent.
アメリカ大陸に住むすべてのアメリカ先住民の中で、プエブロ族が最も古いように思われる。
13 The local people armed themselves and sporadically resisted aggression by the military.
地元の人々は武装して、軍隊による侵攻に散発的に抵抗した。
14 Let's stop complaining about the lack of flexibility in our organization.
組織に柔軟性がないことに不満を言うのはやめよう。

関係節は名詞を修飾します。

15 I'd like to talk to the doctor who made out this prescription.
この処方をした医者に話がしたいのですが。
16 The liquid contains a lot of impurities which may be poisonous.
毒性があるかもしれない不純物をこの液体はたくさん含んでいる。
17 One of the most serious problems that some students have is a lack of motivation.
学生の一部が抱えている最も重大な問題の1つは、やる気がないということだ。
18 The article specifies nothing relevant to the problem we are presently discussing.
その論文は、私たちが今議論している問題に関わることは何も取り上げていない。
19 I've seen countless instances where endeavor was rewarded with success.
努力が成功によって報われた事例を、私は数えきれないほど見てきている。

12-2　副詞的修飾語句

　頻度を表す副詞（always、often、usually など）は、① 動詞の前、② 助動詞の後ろ、③ be 動詞の後ろに置くのが一般的です。状態を表す副詞（fast、easily、well など）は文末に置きますが、頻度を表す副詞と同じ位置に置かれることもあります。また文頭に置くこともあります。文頭では文全体を修飾していることがあります。

1 You are always coughing and look in pain.
あなたはいつも咳をしていて、つらそうに見えます。

2 I've suffered from a terrible headache recently. I'm afraid it may be a sign of a stroke.
   私は最近ひどい頭痛に悩んでいる。脳卒中の兆候ではないかと心配している。
3 At the press conference the police emphasized that they were seriously investigating the case.
   記者会見で警察は、その事件を真剣に捜査していることを強調した。
4 Today, the town is a mere shadow of the former, thriving coal mine town.
   今日ではその町は、炭鉱の町として繁栄していたかつての姿の影にすぎなくなっている。

to 不定詞が動詞を修飾することがあります。

5 I know that you're angry, but please don't hang up because I'm calling to say that I'm sorry.
   あなたが怒っていることはわかりますが、私が悪かったと言うために電話をしているのですから、どうか切らないでください。
6 The mass media conduct public opinion polls to determine what people think about important national issues.
   重要な国家的問題について人々が何を考えているのかを判断するために、マスコミは世論調査を実行する。
7 The man looked sullen from the beginning, and then shook his head to show his disagreement.
   その男は最初から不機嫌に見えて、同意できないことを示すために首を振った。
8 To hear that the tuition would be raised, the student helplessly uttered a sigh of dismay.
   授業料が値上げされることを聞いて、その学生はどうしようもないという風に落胆のため息をついた。

前置詞句が動詞を修飾することがあります。

9 The absence of light means that nothing grows in these dark caves.
   光がないということは、これらの暗い洞穴には何も生えないということだ。
10 Unfortunately, my neighbor lost his job because he didn't show up for work on time.
    気の毒なことに、仕事場に時間通りに行かなかったので、私の隣人は仕事を失った。
11 Cheaper components and increased supply have brought the prices of computers down in recent years.　近年では、部品が安くなり、供給が増加したために、コンピュータの価格が安くなった。
12 I don't know how Mary can care for eleven children without help.
    メアリが援助なしでどうやって11人の子供の面倒をみられるのか、私にはわからない。

時、条件、理由、譲歩などの接続詞によって導入される節は、文全体を修飾します。

Unit 12　形容詞的修飾語句と副詞的修飾語句　101

13 If you'd like to apply for admission, you must fill out this form.
入学の申し込みをするつもりであれば、この書類に記入しなければならない。

14 When he rang home, his cousin answered the phone.
彼が自宅に電話すると、彼のいとこが電話に出た。

15 The court rejected the confession of the defendant because it was given against his will.
被告の自白がその意志に反してなされたものだったので、法廷はその自白を無効とした。

16 Although we can communicate more easily than before, we still have trouble understanding and respecting each other.　以前に比べるとコミュニケーションは簡単になったが、それでもお互いに理解したり尊敬しあったりすることに障害はある。

分詞構文は文全体を修飾します。

17 Realizing that I'd got on the wrong train going in the wrong direction, I leaped off before the door closed.　違う方向に行く違う列車に乗ったことがわかったので、ドアが閉まる前に飛び降りた。

18 Spoken to in an unfamiliar language, I didn't know how to react.
知らない言葉で話しかけられたので、どのように反応したらいいのかわからなかった。

19 Seeing the hardships and pathetic conditions they were suffering, I could not help feeling pity for them.　彼らが被っている困難や痛ましい状況を目にして、私は彼らを気の毒に思う気持ちを抑えられなかった。

20 Admitting that the plan is feasible, I still think it is impractical.
その計画は実行可能だと認めるにしても、私はそれでもそれが現実的ではないと思う。

Exercise　以下の文の形容詞的修飾語句と副詞的修飾語句を示し、それぞれが何を修飾しているか指摘しなさい。

(1) English has practically become the global means of communication.

(2) Many regions in Japan are separated by mountains, so communities, unable to come and go easily, developed their own respective dialects.

(3) Ironically, the student who was always scolded by the teacher for his laziness got the best degree.

(4) Aurelian, the last of those emperors referred to as five good emperors, tried to restore currency stability during his reign.

(5) The ability to recognize individuals can convey significant benefits to social animals.

(6) Europeans began collecting exotic artifacts almost immediately upon discovering the

world beyond Europe.

(7) Scott Hall was an outstanding painter, though he didn't receive the recognition he deserved while he was alive.

(8) The doctrine he refers to in the preface of the book seems arbitrary to me.

(9) Seemingly, the sayings in Matthew 5-7 constitute a single continuous discourse or sermon delivered by Jesus mainly in metaphor.

(10) Chimps have had to assimilate their behavior to the styles predominant in their group.

(11) The municipal government admitted accountability for the random imprisonment of innocent citizens caused by the police.

(12) If you visit the small village located in the valley and go sightseeing, the shrine must be included in your itinerary.

(13) People growing up in different countries will interpret the same phrase in a different way.

(14) In every American community, there are dozens of organizations that depend upon help provided by volunteers.

(15) When we say a person is difficult, this may be a primitive response generated by our own prejudices.

(16) One difficulty in negotiating business across national borders lies in communication problems involving cultural differences.

(17) Your life has the potential to be a wondrous journey filled with exciting moments and astonishing experiences.

(18) The Japanese people living in the middle of the 19th century managed to extricate themselves from a feudal social and political structure.

(19) In one study published last year, a group of people asked to move their eyes in a specific way while puzzling over a logical problem were more likely to solve it.

Unit 13
比　較

　比較とは、性質や状態などについて複数のものを比べることです。英語では「AはBより～だ」や「Aが一番～だ」という意味を表す場合には、用いられる形容詞や副詞が特別の形をとります。

13-1　同等比較

　as ～ as で「～と同じくらい」という意味になります。「～」には形容詞か副詞がきます。否定文、疑問文の場合には、so ～ as になることがあります。同等比較の場合、形容詞や副詞は特別の形をとりませんが、このような同等比較に用いられる形容詞や副詞の単純な形を「原級」と呼びます。

1. Transcribing the manuscript correctly is as difficult as finding a contact lens in the desert because the letters are really illegible.　その手書きの文書を正しく転写することは、文字が全く判読できないので、砂漠でコンタクトレンズを見つけるのと同じくらい難しい。
2. The creature propagates itself as rapidly as mice do.
その生物はネズミが増えるのと同じくらい速く増殖する。
3. Despite common misconceptions, gorillas are as meek an animal as horses.
一般に誤解されているのとは違って、ゴリラは馬と同じくらいおとなしい動物だ。
4. The plan you are suggesting has as many defects as the one we dismissed at the previous conference.　あなたが提案している計画は、前の会議で却下した計画と同じくらい多くの欠点がある。
5. The president wasn't as outspoken as the TV critic when he commented on the subject.
大統領は、その話題についてコメントしたときは、テレビの評論家ほど率直ではなかった。

13-2　比較級・最上級

　「より～な…」という意味を表す比較級を作るためには、形容詞・副詞に -er をつけるか、前に more を置くかのどちらかの方法をとります。「一番～な」という意味の最上級を作る場合には、語尾に -est をつけるか、前に most を置くかのどちらの方法をとります。
　1音節の単語は以下の例のように語尾に -er をつけます。
・long-longer-longest（長い）
・short-shorter-shortest（短い）

・big-bigger-biggest（大きい）
・thick-thicker-thickest（厚い）

　2音節の単語は語尾に -er / -er をつけて比較級・最上級を作るものと、前に more や most を置いて比較級・最上級を作るものがあります。2音節の単語で -er / -est をつけて比較級・最上級を作るのは、語尾が -er / -y / -ow で終わる2音節の形容詞です。
・clever-cleverer-cleverest（頭が良い）
・happy-happier-happiest（幸せな）
・shallow-shallower-shallowest（浅い）

　-ure や -st で終わる形容詞も -er や -est をつけて比較級・最上級を作ることがあります。
・mature-maturer-maturest（成熟した）
・robust-robuster-robustest（がっしりした）

　capable（できる）、common（共通の）、pleasant（楽しい）、handsome（立派な）、secure（確実な）などは -er / -est をつけて比較級・最上級を作ることも、more / most を前置して比較級・最上級を作ることもできます。一般的には more / most がよく使われています。

　上記以外の2音節の単語、及び3音節以上の単語は more / most をつけて比較級・最上級を作ります。early 以外の2音節の副詞は more / most をつけて比較級・最上級を作ることが多くなっています。なお形容詞の最上級は通常定冠詞 the を伴います。

・careful—more careful—most careful（注意深い）
・dangerous—more dangerous—most dangerous（危険な）
・efficient—more efficient—most efficient（効率的な）

★ -er、-est のつけ方
① 語尾に発音しない e があるときには e をとって、er / est をつけます。
・wise-wiser-wisest（賢い）

②「短母音＋子音1文字」で終わるときには子音を重ねます。
・hot-hotter-hottest（暑い）

③「子音＋y」で終わる語は y を取って -ier / -iest をつけます。
・pretty-prettier-prettiest（かわいい）

④ good や bad などのように不規則な変化をするものもあります。
・good / well–better–best（よい）
・bad / ill / badly–worse–worst（悪い、悪く）
・many / much–most–more（多くの）
・little–less–least（小さな）

　比較の対象は than で示します。

Unit 13　比較　　105

Dick is taller than Jack.　ディックはジャックよりも背が高い。
Jenny is more talkative than Claire.　ジェニーはクレアよりもおしゃべりだ。

1. Minute research has shown that cranes in Hokkaido are far <u>more numerous than</u> previously estimated.　詳しい調査をしたところ、北海道のツルは、以前見積もられていたよりもはるかに数が多いことがわかった。
2. Although electricity travels fast, its velocity is finite and over a wire it is <u>slower than</u> in a vacuum.
電気は速く伝わるが、その速度には限りがあって、電線の中では真空中よりも遅くなる。
3. The fighter jets were deployed to the bases <u>earlier than</u> scheduled.
ジェット戦闘機は予定よりも早く基地に配置された。
4. The operation has been worked out <u>more meticulously than</u> the previous ones.
その作戦は、以前の作戦よりも注意深く練り上げられた。
5. Human beings are <u>the most astonishing</u> exception to the broad principle that the life span of mammals correlates with size.
人類は、哺乳類の寿命はその大きさに比例するという一般的な原理に対する最も驚くべき例外だ。
6. The institute analyzed the review of laundry detergent, identifying those that perform <u>best</u> on removing stains and odors.　その研究所は洗濯用洗剤の評価を分析し、汚れやにおいを除去する際に最もよい働きをする洗剤をつきとめた。

13-3　劣等比較

　less を形容詞・副詞の前に置くことで、「より～ではない」という意味を表します。これを「劣等比較」と呼びます。以下に名詞がくる場合は、不可算名詞の前には less、可算名詞複数形の前には fewer を置いて劣等比較の形を作ります。

1. When a child, Rick was <u>less conspicuous than</u> some of the pupils, so nobody imagined he would grow up to be a leading mathematician.
子供の頃、リックは一部の生徒よりは目立たなかったので、大きくなって一流の数学者になるとは誰も想像していなかった。
2. Students nowadays consult a dictionary <u>less often than</u> those more than ten years ago did.
最近の学生は、10年以上前の学生に比べると辞書をひく頻度が少なくなっている。
3. The only advice I can give to those who are on a diet is to take <u>fewer</u> calories.
ダイエットしている人たちに私ができる唯一の助言は、カロリーの摂取を減らすことだ。
4. The best way to prevent arteriosclerosis is to take <u>less</u> salt.
動脈硬化を防ぐ一番よい方法は、塩の摂取を減らすことだ。

13-4　比較対象を to で導入する表現

動詞の prefer（好む）、形容詞の superior（よりすぐれた）や inferior（より劣った）や senior（年上の）や junior（若い）は比較の対象を to で示します。ただし、prefer はそれを rather than で示すことがあります。

1　Some people say that Eastern education is superior to Western education.
　東洋の教育は西洋の教育よりも優れていると言う人もいる。
2　Though Tom is much junior to you, he is equal to this difficult but challenging project.
　トムは君よりずっと若いが、この困難だがやりがいのある計画を実行する能力がある。
3　I prefer losing the game to winning it by cheating.
　ズルをして試合に勝つより負けたほうがよい。

Exercise 1　空所に入れるのに最も適当なものを選んで文を完成させなさい。

(1)　It is ridiculous that it is as cheap to buy a new TV (　) to repair the old one.
(a) than　(b) as　(c) rather　(d) like

(2)　Megumi said that she would arrive (　) than the rest of us since she had something to settle before she departed.
(a) late　(b) latter　(c) later　(d) lately

(3)　This used piano is much (　) than that new one, though I'm not sure about its quality.
(a) least expensive　(b) little expensive　(c) as expense　(d) less expensive

(4)　Nowadays, (　) people go to movie theaters because they prefer to watch DVDs at home.
(a) fewer　(b) little　(c) lesser　(d) smaller

(5)　Diamonds are (　) all substances; they can be cut only by other diamonds.
(a) the hardest of　(b) more than hard　(c) harder of　(d) hardest

(6)　The foods that contain (　) are made of animal fat, whereas vegetables have the least energy.
(a) as much as energy　(b) the more energy　(c) the most energy　(d) higher than energy

(7)　After a brief conversation with Mary, John found he was (　) to her by a year.
(a) adult　(b) mature　(c) older　(d) senior

(8)　If you cannot meet the deadline, we would prefer receiving a late report (　) none at all.
(a) except for　(b) rather than　(c) besides　(d) without

Exercise 2　下線部の中で文法的・語法的に間違いがあるものを1つ選びなさい。

(1)　My friends (a) and I found (b) the new textbook to (c) be easy as (d) the old one.

(2)　One of the (a) ways you (b) can improve your proficiency in English is (c) by reading as (d) many as books as you can.

(3)　Japan is (a) said to be (b) more safe than (c) any other (d) country in the world.

(4)　The (a) continual aftershocks (b) terrified the village (c) inhabitants (d) much more the initial earthquake.

(5)　The number of students who (a) were late (b) for the class was (c) much (d) fewer than I had expected.

(6)　She (a) wore a dress (b) to the party that was (c) far more attractive than (d) the other girls.

(7)　During the music concert, Yoshiko most enjoyed (a) listening to her friend Atsushi's technique, (b) which she thought was (c) more skillful than (d) from other performers.

(8)　(a) Unlike most major art museums, (b) entrance to London's National Gallery, (c) which houses one of the world's (d) most greatest collections of European paintings, is free.

(9)　(a) Most people in this (b) office think the room at the far end of this corridor is (c) best place to work (d) in the building.

(10)　When she goes (a) on vacation, Carol prefers swimming and surfing (b) to (c) lying on the beach and (d) eat ice cream.

13-5　倍数比較

「AのX倍」という意味を表すために、英語では比較表現を使います。

★ X times as ＋形容詞・副詞の原級＋ as ／ X times ＋形容詞・副詞の比較級＋ than

　2倍の場合にはtwiceを用い、3倍以上の場合はthree timesのように「数詞＋times」を用います。半分の場合は「half as ＋原級＋ as A」を用います。また、分数の場合はたとえば「Aの3分の1」は「one third as ＋原級＋ as A」や one third more than A のように、thirdや fourth など「X番目」という意味を表す数詞（序数詞）を使います。

> 1　The brain capacity of a human being is about four times as large as that of a gorilla.
> 　　人間の脳の容量は、ゴリラの脳の容量の約4倍だ。
> 2　Dogs can discriminate odors at concentrations nearly 100 million times lower than humans can.
> 　　イヌは人間と比べて、一億分の一近くの濃度のにおいをかぎ分けられる。

3 People with elevated body temperature perspire a lot, and their pulse is twice as fast as when their temperature is normal. 体温が高いと人間はたくさん汗をかくし、その脈拍も普通の体温の時の2倍になる。
4 Regrettably the benefit we got from the project was only two fifth as large as we had expected.
残念なことに、その事業から我々が得た利益は、予想したものの5分の2にすぎなかった。

13-6　名詞を用いた倍数表現

比較級を用いないで、X times the number of A（AのX倍の数）やX times the size of A（AのX倍の大きさ）のように倍数を表すことができます。そのほかにweight（重さ）、distance（距離）、length（長さ）、depth（深さ）、density（濃さ）、population（人口）などの数量を表す名詞を用いることもできます。

1 The area of the newly discovered ruins is estimated to be three times the size of Tokyo Dome.
新しく発見された遺跡の面積は、東京ドームの3倍あると見積もられている。
2 According to a computation, Pluto has fifty times the specific gravity of the earth.
計算では、冥王星の密度は地球の比重の50倍もあるということだ。
3 The country has more than twice the number of Japan's population.
その国は日本の2倍以上の人口がある。

13-7　その他の覚えておきたい比較表現

よく目にする代表的な比較表現はそのまま覚えておきましょう。

① A is more X than any B ≒ A is as X as any B
「AはどのBよりもXだ」

② No A is more X than B「BよりXなAはない」
No A is as X as B「BほどXなAはない」

③ A is no more B than C is D
　= A is not B any more than C is D
「AがBでないのは、CがDでないのと同じだ」
=「CがDでないようにAはBではない」
（DがBと同じ場合）「AはCと同様にBではない」

④ A is no less B than C is D
「AがBなのは、CがDなのと同じだ」

= 「CがDであるようにAはBだ」
(DがBと同じ場合)「AはCと同様にBだ」

⑤ A is not so much B as (A is) C
　= A is not B so much as (A is) C
　「AはBというよりもむしろCだ」

⑥ The 比較級, the 比較級 「〜であればあるほど…である」

⑦ I would rather A than B
　= I would sooner A than B
　= I would as soon A as B
　「私はAするよりもむしろBしたい」

1. Some animals rely more on their sense of smell than on any other sense.
動物の中には、他のどの感覚よりも嗅覚に頼っているものもいる。

2. The captain is as accountable for the accident as any other crew member.
船長が、他のどの船員よりも事故の責任が大きい。

3. No single idea has dominated Western civilization in modern times (more) than the idea of progress.
進歩という思想ほど、近代の西洋文明を支配した思想はない。

4. In no other city in Japan are old things as well preserved as in Kyoto.
日本の都市で、京都ほど古いものが保存されている都市はない。

5. Nothing hastens the process of social change as much as war, and England in the first half of the twentieth century was deeply involved in two wars more costly and more destructive than any other in history.　戦争ほど社会の変化を急速に進めるものはない。そして20世紀前半のイギリスは、歴史上他のどの戦争に比べても、犠牲が大きく破壊的な2つの戦争に深く関与した。

6. When it comes to sewing, you are no more dexterous than I am.
裁縫になると、あなたは私と同じくらい不器用だ。

7. The man can no more help being outstanding among ordinary people than gold can among pennies.　その男は、普通の人々の中にいるとどうしても目立ってしまう。それは、ペニーの中で金貨が目立つのと同じだ。

8. The amusement park is no less appealing to adults than it is to children.
その遊園地は、子供だけでなく大人も楽しむことができる。

9. What you proposed sounds to me not so much like a feasible plan as a castle built in the air.
あなたが提案したことは実行可能な計画というよりも、むしろ砂上の楼閣に聞こえる。

10 One of the most important factors in adjusting to a new culture is the age at which a person goes abroad. The more years they spent in their own countries, the harder it is to accept new patterns of life.
新しい文化に適応する際に最も重要な要因は、人が外国に行く年齢だ。自分の国で年月を長く過ごせば過ごすほど、新しい生活様式を受けいれるのが難しくなる。

11 Young entrepreneurs who come up with innovative ideas would rather go to Tokyo than stay in Osaka.　革新的な考えを手に入れた若い企業家たちは、大阪にとどまるよりも東京に行きたがる。

Exercise 3　空所に入れるのに最も適当なものを選んで文を完成させなさい。

(1)　A fuel cell could be (　　) as a lead acid battery, but, even today, it is too heavy and costly.
(a) as strong twice　(b) as twice strong　(c) twice strong so　(d) twice as strong

(2)　Aerogel is the lightest solid material known, with a density only three times (　　) of air.
(a) that　(b) this　(c) it　(d) than

(3)　Dan Carter, an outstanding fly-half for the Crusaders, scored more penalty goals than (　　) in the season.
(a) any kickers　(b) any other kicker　(c) all the kickers　(d) all kicker.

(4)　Susan loves video games. She enjoys (　　) into the role of a video game character.
(a) nothing more than slipping　(b) anything more than to slip
(c) something more than slipping　(d) everything more than to slip

(5)　I cannot change his mind (　　) I can turn a stone into bread.
(a) more than　(b) any more than　(c) no more than　(d) not more than

(6)　Animals learn by trial and error, and the smarter they are, the (　　) trials they need.
(a) many　(b) much　(c) less　(d) fewer

(7)　Due to the economic crisis, (　　) than ten banks were forced to close down.
(a) not lower　(b) not larger　(c) no more　(d) no fewer

(8)　Your idea is (　　) than mine. In fact it is slightly better.
(a) greater　(b) no better　(c) no worse　(d) worse

(9)　A man's worth is to be estimated not so much by his social position (　　) by his character.

(a) as (b) as well (c) rather (d) than

Unit 14
仮 定 法

　仮定法は、現実のものとは限らず、起こる可能性がある（あった）だけの事柄を表すための動詞の形です。仮定法の基本は「XならばY」という条件部と帰結部の組み合わせです。この形の条件文のXを条件節、Yを帰結節と呼びます。

14-1　仮定法過去
　仮定法過去とは、現在の事実とは異なること、あるいは近い未来のありそうにないことを仮定し、もしそうならどうなるかを表します。

If I had wings, I could fly to her.
私に翼があれば、彼女のところへ飛んでいけるのに。

　実際には私には翼がありませんが、「もし翼があれば」と現在の事実に反する仮定を立てます。if節（条件節）の述語動詞は過去形になります。be動詞の場合にはwereを用います。主節（帰結節）は「主語＋助動詞の過去形＋動詞の原形」という形をとります。ここではcouldが用いられていますが、意味に応じてcould以外にwould / should / mightなどが用いられます。また、条件節にbe動詞が用いられている場合、ifを省略して、主語とbe動詞を倒置させることで、条件節を作れます。

1　If he knew how I suffered, he would pity me.
　　私が苦しんでいることを知っていれば、彼は私に同情するだろう。
2　If taxes were raised again, the economy would fall into a long-term recession.
　　また税金が上がったら、経済が長期にわたる不況に陥るだろう。
3　Were you familiar with the mechanism of the modern economy, you would not make such a risky investment.
　　現在の経済のしくみをよく知っていたら、そんな危険な投資はしないだろう。

14-2　仮定法過去完了
　仮定法過去完了は、過去の事実に反する仮定を立て、もしそうならどうなったであろうかということを表します。

If I had studied hard, I would have passed the exam.
もし一生懸命勉強していたら、試験に合格していただろう。

　実際には一生懸命勉強していなかったのですが「もし一生懸命勉強していたら」と過去

の事実に反することを仮定しています。if 節の中の動詞は過去完了形になります。帰結節の動詞は「主語＋助動詞の過去形＋have＋過去分詞」という形をとります。仮定法過去完了では、if を省略し、主語と had を倒置させることで条件節を作ることができます。

1 If you had attended the intensive course, you would have gotten a better grade.
集中コースをとっていたら、あなたはもっとよい成績をとることができただろうに。
2 If they had been aware of the recklessness of the plan, they wouldn't have gone ahead with it.
彼らがその計画の無謀さを知っていたら、それを進めることはなかっただろう。
3 Had I compared the prices of the computer at different stores, I could have saved some money.
いろいろな店でコンピュータの値段を比較していたら、いくらかお金が節約できただろう。
4 Had she been more modest, more men would have wooed her.
彼女がもっと控えめだったら、もっと多くの男が彼女に言い寄っただろう。

14-3　If 仮定法過去完了，仮定法過去

　過去の事実に反する仮定を立て、その結果今こうなっているだろうという意味を表す場合、if 節の中を過去完了形にし、帰結節は「主語＋助動詞の過去形＋動詞の原形」という、仮定法過去の形を用います。

If you had not rescued me, I would not be alive now.
もしあなたが私を救出していなかったならば、私は今生きてはいないだろう。

　実際には、あなたが私を救出したので、私は生きています。このように過去の事実に反する仮定を表す場合は、if 節の中が had not rescued のように過去完了形になり、帰結節は現在の事実に反する事柄を表しているので I would not be のように「主語＋助動詞の過去形＋動詞原形」という仮定法過去の形になっています。まれに「If 仮定法過去，仮定法過去完了」という形もあります。

1 If he had carefully read the instructions written on the box, he would not be injured now.
彼が箱の上に書かれていた指示を注意して読んでいたら、今頃怪我をしてなどいないだろうに。
2 Had the politician not been involved in the scandal, he would be a minister now.
その政治家が醜聞に巻き込まれていなかったら、今頃は大臣になっているだろう。

14-4　if 節中に should や were to do を用いる仮定法

　未来に起こる可能性が低いことを表すためには、If 節の中に should を用いるか、あるいは If S were to do という形を用います。どちらの場合も、接続詞 if を使わないで、主語と should あるいは、主語と were を倒置させて、条件節を作ることができます。また should の場合、帰結節の助動詞が過去形にならないことがあります。

（注）　未来のありそうにないことを仮定する場合に用いると説明される場合もありますが、実際には普通に起きると予想されることについても用いられています。

> 1　If the female comedian should succeed in climbing Mt. Everest, how will people react?
>   その女性タレントがエベレストに登ることに成功したら、人々はどのような反応をするだろうか。
> 2　Should you lose your way in the middle, try to contact me on your cell phone.
>   途中で道に迷ったら、携帯電話で私に連絡してみてください。
> 3　If I were to win the lottery, I would spend the money traveling around the world.
>   もし宝くじに当たったら、そのお金を使って世界一周をしたい。
> 4　Were you to run for governor, what would you like to talk about?
>   あなたが知事に立候補するとすれば、何について話したいですか。

Exercise 1　空所に入れるのに最も適当なものを選んで文を完成させなさい。

(1)　If I (　　) a little more time after school every day, I'd like to have a part time job.
(a) had　(b) had had　(c) have had　(d) would have had

(2)　If Americans ate fewer foods with sugar and salt, their general health (　　) better.
(a) be　(b) is　(c) will be　(d) would be

(3)　If I (　　) Jun was in the hospital, I most certainly would have gone to visit him and brought him some flowers or fruits.
(a) could know　(b) knew　(c) had known　(d) would have known

(4)　We lost the game, but we (　　) won if one of our players hadn't been hurt.
(a) might have been　(b) might well have　(c) might well　(d) may have

(5)　(　　) more as a student, I would not be what I am now
(a) If I study　(b) If I studied　(c) If I would study　(d) If I had studied

(6)　(　　) I in your place, I wouldn't endorse such a risky loan.
(a) Be　(b) Been　(c) Was　(d) Were

(7)　(　　) there been a way for me to relieve them of their predicament, I would have done everything in my power.

(a) But　(b) If　(c) Had　(d) Once

(8)　If the sun (　　) go around the moon, Arthur would never abandon hope.
(a) can　(b) should not　(c) will　(d) were to

(9)　(　　) you have any questions, please don't hesitate to contact us.
(a) Would　(b) Should　(c) Could　(d) Might

(10) (　　) a mega-quake to hit as is presumed it will within thirty years, most of the nuclear power plants couldn't stay standing and core meltdowns would be spawned.
(a) If　(b) Should　(c) Unless　(d) Were

14-5　were it not for と had it not been for

　if it were not for ～（～がなければ）と if it had not been for ～（～がなかったならば）では、if を省略にして倒置しても、同じ意味を表すことができます。それぞれ were it not for ～、had it not been for ～ になります。without ～ と but for ～ などの前置詞句で同じ意味を表すこともできます。

1　If it were not for the sun, no creature could live.
　　太陽がなければ、どんな生物も生きていけないだろう。
2　If it had not been for the infusion of capital by the government, the company would have gone bankrupt.
　　政府による資本注入がなかったら、その会社は倒産していただろう。
3　Had it not been for the war, the bilateral relationship wouldn't have gotten sour.
　　その戦争がなかったら、両国の関係が険悪になることはなかっただろう。
4　Without the invention of microchips, computers couldn't be this compact.
　　マイクロチップが発明されなかったとしたら、コンピュータはこれほど軽量にはなっていないだろう。
5　With your precious advice, we could have gotten through the difficult phase.
　　あなたの貴重な助言があれば、困難な局面を乗り切ることができたでしょう。

14-6　その他の仮定法を用いる主な表現

　定型となっている仮定法表現をいくつか覚えましょう。

① I wish / if only S did　「～であればいいのに」
　 I wish / if only S had done　「～であったらよかったのに」

② as if + S did　「～であるかのように」
　 as if + S had done　「～であったかのように」
（注）　実際には as if 節の中に直説法が用いられる場合も珍しくはありません。

③ I'd rather S did 「Sにむしろ〜してもらいたい」
④ It's time S did 「Sが〜するべき時だ」

1. I wish I were smart enough to crack the cipher.
　この暗号を解けるくらい自分の頭がよければいいのだが。
2. If only you had been there to celebrate that occasion.
　あなたがそこにいて、その機会を祝うことができたらよかったのですが。
3. I felt as if the door to the achievement of what I envisioned were being shut.
　私が思い描いていたものを達成するための扉が閉じられつつあるかのように感じられた。
4. The children looked feeble as if they had not eaten anything for days.
　その子供たちは何日も何も食べていないかのように弱って見えた。
5. I'd rather you didn't persist in that ridiculous idea.
　あなたにはそんな馬鹿げた考えに固執しないでもらいたいものだ。
6. It's time you stopped trying to save face.　面目を保とうとするのはもうやめる時だ。

14-7　仮定法現在

　要求、提案、命令、主張、推薦、決定、願望、依頼など、まだ現実には起きていない事柄を表す動詞や名詞などに支配されるthat節の中では、「should＋動詞」か「動詞の原形」が用いられます。これを仮定法現在と言います。

① 仮定法現在をとる代表的な動詞にはdemand（要求する）、require（要求する）、request（要請する）、suggest（提案する）、propose（提案する）、order（命令する）、command（命令する）、insist（主張する）、recommend（推薦する）、decide（決定する）、ask（お願いする）などがあります。すべてまだ実現していない内容を表します。

② あとに続くthat節の中で仮定法現在が用いられる代表的な名詞にdemand（要求）、suggestion（提案）、proposal（提案）、order（命令）、command（命令）、recommendation（推薦）などがあります。

③ あとに続くthat節の中に仮定法現在をとる代表的な形容詞にessential（不可欠な）、anxious（切望する）、desirous（切望する）があります。また、on condition that...（…という条件で）もthat節で仮定法現在をとることもあります（直説法も用いられます）。

1. The police ordered that all windows be shut.
　警察はすべての窓を閉めるように命じた。
2. One of my colleagues suggested that the project be modified so that its cost would be brought down within the budget.　私の同僚の1人は、その計画を修正して、経費が予算内に収まるように減額するように提案した。
3. People world over are anxious that the dispute in the region would be peacefully solved.

その地域の紛争が平和的に解決されることを全世界の人々が切望している。

Exercise 2　空所に入れるのに最も適当なものを選んで文を完成させなさい。

(1)　If (　) were not for the super-computer that enables us to calculate almost infinitely faster, the experiment would take weeks to complete.
(a) only　(b) there　(c) any　(d) it

(2)　(　) for your advice, I would not have succeeded in my attempt to persuade my boss to give a green light to the project.
(a) Were it not　(b) Had it not been　(c) Were there not　(d) Had there not been

(3)　Without Chinese influence, Japanese culture (　) what it is today.
(a) are not　(b) had not been　(c) were not　(d) would not be

(4)　I worked part time and put aside most of the money I earned. (　), I couldn't have afforded the trip.
(a) Otherwise　(b) Nevertheless　(c) For this　(d) Therefore

(5)　A Japanese (　) in a different way, shying away from confrontation.
(a) had reacted　(b) will have reacted　(c) will react　(d) would have reacted

(6)　I'm disappointed with the result because we (　) the game against the team last night.
(a) could have won　(b) could win　(c) should be winning　(d) should win

(7)　Too bad it's already been completed. I would (　) to watch you paint it stroke by stroke.
(a) have liked　(b) like to　(c) have missed　(d) like to enjoy

(8)　This equation is too complicated to work out in my mind. If (　) I had a computer here.
(a) better　(b) wish　(c) could　(d) only

(9)　I wish I (　) to Germany to study cutting-edge technology for genetic modification when I was given the chance to several years ago.
(a) could go　(b) would go　(c) could have gone　(d) must have gone

(10)　I wish that man (　) tapping his fingers on the desk. It's really annoying.
(a) has stopped　(b) would stop　(c) stop　(d) stopping

(11)　I would much rather you (　) hit at the keyboard in this room. It really gets on my nerves.

(a) might not (b) cannot (c) didn't (d) wouldn't

(12) He speaks as if he (　　) everything about cyber-crime.
(a) to know (b) knew (c) known (d) knowing

(13) My foot feels (　　) it were suffering a fracture.
(a) as if (b) as much as (c) so that (d) such as

(14) It's about time you (　　) considering your future seriously.
(a) start (b) started (c) starts (d) will starts

(15) My teacher recommended that we (　　) at least two books a month in the originals.
(a) read (b) are reading (c) have read (d) may read

(16) The hotel guest demanded that a bellman (　　) to his room at once.
(a) be sent (b) sending (c) sent (d) would be sent

(17) Railroad companies request that passengers (　　) on cell phones while riding on the train.
(a) don't to talk (b) to not talk (c) not talking (d) not talk

(18) The doctor's recommendation was (　　) be in the hospital for another week.
(a) for me (b) if I'll (c) me to (d) that I

(19) It is essential that freedom of expression (　　) secured in the newly forming democracy after the constitution is approved by the end of next year.
(a) has been (b) could be (c) had been (d) be

Unit 15
倒置、要素の移動、強調、省略

15-1　倒置

否定の副詞、not を含む副詞句、副詞節、only を含む副詞、副詞節が文頭にくると、主語と助動詞の倒置が起きます。

1　Little did I dream that the small fault of the design would result in the collapse of the bridge.
設計の小さな失敗が橋の崩壊という結果を引き起こすとは夢にも思っていなかった。

2　Not once had the general doubted the fidelity of his men.
将軍は自分の部下の忠誠心を一度も疑ったことはなかった。

3　Not until the island sank completely under the sea did people realize the seriousness of the effects of global warming.　島が完全に海中に沈んでやっと、人々は地球温暖化の影響の重大さがわかった。

4　Only at dawn did we find our way to the remote village.
夜明けになってやっと、その遠く離れた村にたどりついた。

5　Only when you ruin your health will the significance of being healthy be brought home to you.
健康を損なってはじめて、健康であることの大切さが身にしみてわかるだろう。

強調するために副詞が文頭にくると、倒置が用いられることがあります。また「The 比較級, the 比較級」の構文で倒置が用いられることもあります。

6　Well should the government know how to react to any kind of contingency.
どんな種類の緊急事態にも対応する方法を政府はよく知っていなければならない。

7　The louder the CD is played, the more clearly can you hear the noise.
CD の音量を上げれば上げるほど、ノイズがはっきり聞こえるようになる。

相手の発言に応じて「私もそうです」と言う場合、肯定文では「so ＋倒置」、否定文では「neither / nor ＋倒置」という形が用いられます。

8　A : I'm unwilling to attend that boring meeting.
　　B : So am I.
　　A : その退屈な会合に私は出たくない。
　　B : 私もそうです。

9　A : I expected that the prosecutors would give up appealing to the high court.

B : <u>So did I.</u>
   A : 検察は高等裁判所に控訴するのをあきらめるだろうと思っていました。
   B : 私もそうです。

10 A : I cannot understand the mindset of people who object to the rule.
   B : <u>Neither can I.</u>
   A : そのルールに反対する人の気持ちは理解できません。
   B : 私もそうです。

11 A : I'm not ambitious to get promoted in this company.
   B : <u>Nor am I.</u>
   A : 私はこの会社で昇進することをそれほど強く望んではいません。
   B : 私もそうです。

15-2 要素の移動

　文を構成する要素としては、主語（S）、目的語（O）、動詞（V）、補語（C）、副詞的修飾句（M）があります。通常は主語（S）が文頭に置かれて、次に動詞（V）がくる語順がとられますが、それ以外の要素を強調したり、長い語句が前に置かれるのを避けたりするために、要素が通常の位置から移動することがあります。

① SVM → MVS
② SVC → CVS
③ SVO → OSV
④ SVOM → SVMO
⑤ SVOC → SVCO

(a) 強調したい要素を文頭に置くことがあります。
(b) 主語が長くなる場合に、MVS、CVS という語順をとることがあります。
(c) 目的語が長くなる場合に SVMO、SVCO という語順になることがあります。
(d) OSV で O の前に否定語がくると倒置が起きます。

1　Across those mountains lies my hometown, which I left ten years ago.
　　この山脈の向こうに私の故郷がある。私はそこを 10 年前に出た。
2　So strong is his decision that it is impossible for us to persuade him not to quit the job.
　　彼の決意は強いので、仕事を辞めないように説得することは不可能だ。
3　Not an intentional falsification of the date did we find in the thesis.
　　その論文に、日付の意図的な改ざんを 1 つも発見することはできなかった。
4　Your other sock is in the doll's bed, and that it got there by itself I do not believe for one moment.　あなたの靴下の片方は人形のベッドにあるが、それがひとりでにそこに

行ったなどと、私は全く信じない。
5 We should immediately put on the table the subject we will have to discuss sooner or later.
そのうちには議論しなければならない話題に、すぐに取りかかるべきだ。
6 Instead of trying to make sure that all children get only those experiences we think are good for them, I would rather make available to children a wide possible range of experiences. すべての子供が、彼らにとって有益だと思われる経験だけをするように配慮しようとするのではなく、できるだけ幅広い範囲の経験を子供たちができるようにするのがよいと思う。

15-3 強調構文
① 強調構文の基礎

It is X that ... という形でXを強調するのが強調構文です。強調構文で強調されるのは、文の主語、目的語、または副詞です。例として I met Sandra yesterday.（私は昨日サンドラに会った）という文で考えましょう。この文からは以下の3つの強調構文を作ることができます。

(a) 主語を強調→ It was I that met Sandra yesterday.
(b) 目的語を強調→ It was Sandra that I met yesterday.
(c) 副詞を強調→ It was yesterday that I met Sandra.

強調構文で強調されるものを強調構文の「焦点」と言います。(a) は I、(b) は Sandra、(c) は yesterday が焦点です。

(a) (b) の that は品詞としては関係代名詞で、(a) は who、(b) は who か whom に置き換えることができます。(c) の that は接続詞なので、which には置き換えられません。It was the illness that made her weak.（彼女を弱くしたのは病気だ）のように、ものを表す名詞が強調されている場合には、that は which に置き換えることができます。強調構文の that はすべて省略可能です。ただし、that が関係代名詞で (a) のように主語として使われる場合も省略されることはありますが、実際の文章ではこの省略はほとんどないようです。強調される副詞としては単独の副詞以外に、副詞句、副詞節などもあります。

1 It is not the quantity of years one lives that matters, but the quality one puts into the quantity.
大切なのは生きている年月の長さではなくて、その長さに与える質なのだ。
2 It is an exact rendering of the interior the mirror reflects.
鏡が映すのは、室内の正確な姿だ。
3 It is at this point that most victims find that they've been deceived by the swindler.

ほとんどの被害者がその詐欺師にだまされていたとわかるのは、まさにその時だ。
4 <u>It was</u> because Dr. Salk developed the vaccine <u>that</u> polio has virtually been eradicated throughout the world.
ポリオが全世界でほぼ撲滅されたのは、ソーク博士がワクチンを開発したおかげだ。

② 疑問詞＋強調構文

疑問詞疑問文の疑問詞を強調するには、「疑問詞＋is it that...?」という構文にします。

1 <u>What was it that</u> upset you so much?
君をそんなに当惑させているのは一体何なんだ。
2 <u>What is it (that)</u> you are trying to protect so ardently?
君がそんなに熱心に守ろうとしているのは何なのだ。
3 <u>When was it that</u> we became aware of the earth warming up?
地球温暖化に私たちが気づいたのは一体いつのことだったろうか。
4 <u>Where was it that</u> they concealed the treasures?
一体どこに彼らは宝を隠したのだろうか。
5 <u>How was it (that)</u> Newton discovered the law of gravity?
ニュートンはどのようにして万有引力の法則を発見したのだろうか。

15-4 省略

前に出てきたのと同じ語句が使われていることがわかる場合には、同じ語句の反復を避けるために省略されることがあります。省略が起こる条件として以下のことを覚えておきましょう。

① 反復を避けるために動詞を省略することがある。
② 主節以外の be 動詞が省略されることがある。
③ 反復を避けるために、to 不定詞の to 以下を省略することがある。
④ 反復を避けるために主語＋述語動詞を省略することがある。
⑤ not だけで否定の副詞節や返答の文の代用になることがある。

1 Jack would have taken what job he could then.
そのとき、ジャックは就ける仕事であれば何にでも就いただろう。
2 If you asked me whether Pat is trustworthy, I'd say he is.
パットが信頼できるかどうか君に尋ねられたら、信頼できると言うだろう。
3 Whoever else may be truant, you mustn't be.
他の誰が怠け者であるとしても、君はそうであってはならない。
4 The president should implement his pledges as we expect him to.
大統領は私たちが期待しているように公約を実行しなければならない。

5　The defendant looked more remorseful about the crime he committed than he really was.
　　その被告は、本心よりも、自分の犯した犯罪を後悔しているように見えた。
6　The prince talked to Cinderella but not to her sisters.
　　王子はシンデレラには話しかけたが、彼女の姉妹には話しかけなかった。
7　I wonder if Kate is coming or not.　ケイトは来るのか来ないのかどっちだろうか。
8　"Did James really say such a stupid thing?" "I think not."
　　「ジェイムズが本当にそんな馬鹿げたことを言ったのか」「言わなかったと思う」

Exercise　空所に入れるのに最も適当なものを選んで文を完成させなさい。

(1)　(　) did Sam realize that he had left his bag at the store.
(a) After he had gotten on the bus　(b) Only after getting on the bus
(c) Upon getting on the bus　(d) When he got on the bus

(2)　Not until 1945 (　) to attend four-year colleges in that country.
(a) did women allowed　(b) no women allowed
(c) were women allowed　(d) women were not allowed

(3)　Included in the price (　) the shipping and handling charges for these items.
(a) do　(b) does　(c) is　(d) are

(4)　On the wall of the study (　) was among the first settlers to come to this area more than three centuries ago.
(a) of the mayor's portrait hanging　(b) a portrait hung of whom the mayor
(c) hung a portrait of the mayor who　(d) with hanging the mayor's portrait

(5)　"I was deeply moved by the courageous deed of the boy." "(　)."
(a) So did I　(b) I did so　(c) So was I　(d) I was so

(6)　"I can't bring myself to climb such a steep mountain." "(　)."
(a) Neither can I　(b) I can't too　(c) Me too　(d) So I can.

(7)　"I hear that you are going to undergo surgery to remove a colonic polyp." "(　)"
(a) So I do　(b) So do I　(c) So I am　(d) So am I

(8)　It (　) John who was held responsible for the article.
(a) became　(b) came　(c) seemed　(d) was

(9)　It's Dad's computer that there is something wrong (　), not mine.
(a) by　(b) of　(c) outside　(d) with

(10) It (　) the Titanic sank while crossing the Atlantic Ocean.
(a) is 1912 when (b) which was in 1912 (c) in 1912 that (d) was in 1912 that

(11) (　) was while you were away that I had words with the neighbor.
(a) It (b) There (c) Such (d) So

(12) What is it about flying that (　) you so much?
(a) scare (b) scares (c) scaring (d) scary

(13) (　) your sweater inside out?
(a) How come it is for you wearing (b) How is it feeling by wearing
(c) On what grounds is it of you to wear (d) Why is it that you wear

(14) He spoke of it as one might (　) a religious experience.
(a) in (b) of (c) to (d) with

(15) The committee did not think that Mike was quite as qualified for the scholarship as the successful candidate (　).
(a) did (b) does (c) was (d) would

(16) Some investors are worried by the news, but they (　) be.
(a) couldn't (b) hadn't (c) mightn't (d) shouldn't

(17) The report was very critical and was clearly (　).
(a) intended (b) intended for (c) intended to be (d) intending to

(18) I hope Anna passed her exam. (　), she'll have to repeat her senior year.
(a) If not (b) With them (c) If so (d) Without them

(19) She spoke good English, (　) with a Japanese accent.
(a) because (b) if (c) though (d) when

(20) I don't discriminate against women, and I (　).
(a) never have (b) have never (c) not have (d) had not

大学生のための 英文法再入門

● 2014 年 11 月 1 日 初版発行 ●
● 2023 年 10 月 31 日 2 刷発行 ●

● 編著者 ●
町田健＋豊島克己
© Ken Machida＋Katsumi Toyoshima, 2014

● 発行者 ●
吉田　尚志

● 発行所 ●
株式会社　研究社
〒102-8152　東京都千代田区富士見 2-11-3
電話　営業 03-3288-7777 (代)
　　　編集 03-3288-7711 (代)
振替　00150-9-26710
https://www.kenkyusha.co.jp/

● 印刷所・本文レイアウト ●
図書印刷株式会社

● 装丁 ●
寺澤　彰二

● 英文校閲 ●
Christopher Belton

ISBN 978-4-327-42193-9　C1082　Printed in Japan

KENKYUSHA
〈検印省略〉